I'm Here For The Girls

By: Renata A. Hannans

THE HOPE DEALER

For interviews or any inquiries pertaining to the content of this publication, please contact the author and publisher directly.

*Each story was authentically told and composed, with permission, based on firsthand contact with all subjects from their reflective accounts of personal experiences.

Email: contact@renatahannans.com

Facebook.com/PSNeverGiveUpHope

Instagram: @RenataHannans

Published via Hope Publishing

www.renatahannans.com

Edited and Formatted by: *iWrite4orU*

Cover Design: The Logo Queen Jax

ISBN: 978-0-578-81583-1

LCCN: 2020923761

Printed in the United States of America

Dedication

To Sweet Grammie and Orain Benjamin Reddick who are both in heaven looking down, this is for you.

To every little girl I have ever met in my work, especially at the Duval Regional Detention Center in Jacksonville, Florida, aka "Hotel", you all have been my driving force for years.

To Ms. Yolanda and Mrs. Nikki, "Thank You" just simply isn't enough. I appreciate you two ladies more than words can express and am forever grateful to God for connecting us.

To Shara, Nisey, Roteia, Emerald, Kenitra, Lola, Tiffany, Jhody, Amanda, Anonymous and Shawneequa: thank you for co-authoring this book with me. You ladies mean more to me than you will ever know. I pray that this book aids you in your healing process from past trauma and that your stories change lives. I love you all and I pray every day that God's will be done in each of your lives.

To the girls and women who will read this, I want you to know that you are loved. You are worthy. You are more than enough. I pray this book touches you deeply.

I'm Here For The Girls

Love,

Renata
THE HOPE DEALER

Foreword

By: Jamila T. Davis

I t's rare in life when you meet someone whose passion for their profession is so electrifying. From behind bars when I connected with Renata Hannans, instantly I knew she was the real deal! For months we shared letters and books that inspired me. I was intrigued to hear about the work she was doing in the free-world, giving a voice to individuals who were incarcerated, such as myself.

I remember the first time I Skyped with Renata as if it were yesterday. It was a cold day in 2016 at the Alderson Federal Prison Camp in Alderson, West Virginia. I combed my hair, put on my uniform, grabbed my coat and headed down to the email room. As I walked down the long, windy hill to my Skype visit, I couldn't help but to imagine if the face I'd see would match with the letters I'd read for months. The time finally arrived—a cheerful, beautiful, brown face appeared on the screen, and I quickly picked up the receiver to talk. From the moment we exchanged words, it became official; I knew Renata would be a person I would support for a long time to come.

As our Skype calls became more regular, I knew she'd be someone I'd consider more like family than a friend. For hours we collaborated about our goals, dreams and missions, and we didn't delay in taking action. I began to share my story and I connected Renata with other women in prison to tell their stories, too. Quickly, our Skype calls became anticipated visits. Each time we spoke, our plans and dreams became larger and clearer. Renata gave me hope. She took me out of the box I was trapped in, reminded me of who I was destined to become and gave me permission to dream again. That meant everything!

Women behind bars is often a population that goes unnoticed. Many have no clue who we are, nor the challenges we face. Back in 2008, I was sentenced to twelve-and-a-half years in Federal prison for bank fraud. I received one of the lengthiest sentences heard of for the crime I committed. At the time, I could see no ending. Truthfully, I wanted to close my eyes and die, until I figured out my fate had tremendous meaning. My life changed when I discovered there was purpose in my pain.

It was in one of the most uncomfortable moments in life that I gained my closest relationship with God. My ability to go within, do the inner work and change my perspective brought me freedom, even behind bars. Instead of focusing on my own problems, I began to closely look at the blaring injustices within the system and I made a vow to become a part of the solution.

While incarcerated, I became an activist. I used my story and the stories of others to shed light on the epidemic of women in prison and the lengthy sentences many of us serve as first-time, nonviolent offenders. I began to write as my life depended on it, and my writing gained light in the free-world. It was through my writing that I was introduced to Renata. She read my story and decided she wanted to help me. Learning about the work she was doing in the field of juvenile justice fueled me to fight even harder to help women like myself who were incarcerated.

In June 2017, I was finally released from prison. One of the first faces I got to see in the free-world was Renata's. It was an incredibly joyous moment to connect the face I saw on the screen with her in person. It was even more gratifying to watch her continue to do the work she so passionately spoke about. When Renata asked me to write this foreword, I was honored. The work she is doing is so meaningful and necessary for our culture. Lots of times, when people hear the stories of credible messengers, it makes them think twice before committing crimes. Learning the severe consequences of criminal behavior is an essential element of crime prevention. In my opinion, it can save so many lives. Therefore, it is my prayer that this book gets in the hands of millions of individuals across the world. May it touch lives just as potently as Renata has touched mine!

Prologue

The Girls

Becoming a mother at the tender age of fourteen made Shara a woman before her time. Never having a relationship with her biological father shaped all of her future relationships with men. At the age of eighteen, she found herself pregnant with her second child and charged with the father's death. Shortly after giving birth, Shara was arrested, convicted and sentenced to life in prison. Today, Shara is still fighting for her freedom as a law clerk in the Florida state prison system.

Born and raised in Port Au Prince, Haiti, with both her mother and father, Nisey's childhood was considered to be normal. However, when she moved to Florida in middle school, her life made a turn for the worse when her father began molesting her. She ended up in Florida's foster care system, where she thrived off of negative attention from men, sought comfort in alcohol and drugs, but lost herself. She is currently serving a fifteen-year sentence.

Roteia was raised by her grandparents, but always wanted to live with her mother. Around age fourteen, she started acting out in hopes that she could go and live with her mom. At age fifteen, she met her then-boyfriend, "Tony", whom she thought was the love of her life. At eighteen, once Tony was released from jail, the two lovebirds were inseparable. Then, one day, Roteia, Tony, and some friends decided to commit a robbery and someone ended up dead...

At a very young age, Emerald and her sister, Christina, were removed from their mother's care. Emerald never saw her mother again after moving to Florida with her father. After years of abuse at the hands of her father, Emerald was placed in foster care, where she fell in love with the streets and everything that came with it. Never having felt loved at home, Emerald sought love in all the wrong places. At fifteen, she was accused of murder and is serving a forty-year sentence.

As a tenured employee of the Jacksonville Sheriff's Office, wife and mother, Kenitra never imagined that prison would be a part of her life. One day, while at work, her estranged ex-husband inquired about a narcotics detective. Kenitra confirmed for him the identity of an undercover officer, which violated job policy and, unbeknownst to her, the law.

Drugs had always been a part of Lola's world. As a child, both of her parents battled and overcame addiction. She began to hate drugs, but was also intrigued by them. At eighteen, she met and fell in love with Tommy, who introduced her to the other side of the game. This is a real-life tale of love and drugs.

Tiffany shares her testimony as one of the youngest women from Florida's death row. Her childhood experiences with men, drugs, and alcoholism played a major role in her decisions. She was charged and convicted of first-degree murder with her boyfriend at the time and two others. Tiffany is now the "Grace Messenger" and uses her testimony to bring others closer to Christ.

As a child with weight insecurities and low self-esteem, Jhody experienced bullying at an early age. After her parents divorced and her father was no longer in the home, Jhody's interest in boys peaked. It wasn't long before a pill addiction led to poor choices. Jhody served eight years in prison and became a law clerk on the inside. Her entire life she has made something out of nothing, and prison was no different.

At age nine, Amanda encountered sexual abuse at the hands of a family member and kept it to herself for years. In middle school, her mom went to prison and she became the mother of the house, figuratively. While Dad worked all the time to provide, she was home raising her siblings and became a mother herself at age fifteen. In order to make ends meet, Amanda started selling drugs and lived much of her youth in and out of jail. Today, she has turned her life around, living for her children after being released from Federal prison in 2017.

"Now faith is the substance of things hope for, the evidence of things unseen." – (Hebrews 11:1)

It has been 20 years since the tragic night that ended the life of her then husband, which catapulted a committed walk of faith. This contributor anonymously shares her journey and two-decade fight to freedom.

Chapter 11: Shawneequa   **Page 93**

From age 13 to 18, Shawneequa served time in a juvenile facility, as she felt that was safer than being home with her abusive, alcoholic mother. Never knowing her real father and being violated by several men in her life made her lose trust in men. After years of failed attempts to get her life together, she finally relocated and things were starting to look up. Six months after relocation, she and her boyfriend were pulled over and arrested on drug charges. Shawneequa was released from a Texas prison in July of 2020 on parole and is now picking up the pieces of her life.

Epilogue

Poem

About the Author

Prologue

S ome may wonder where my passion in the criminal justice system stems from. In high school, my friend, Lissa, worked in a summer program at the Duval County Courthouse and she advised me that anyone can attend court hearings. So, I started attending court proceedings and trials and instantly became hooked at age sixteen. I became familiar with due process and I observed the injustices firsthand. I never knew what career field I would end up in, but I knew I wanted to help people who were incarcerated. From this seed planted by my friend, I would spend a lot of time in courtrooms over the years, unbeknownst to me.

This newly-discovered passion was further ignited while I was assigned to work closely with at-risk high school students and was an eye-witness to the school-to-prison pipeline; it is a very real concept. A prime example includes children coming to school for an array of reasons; they get into trouble, and eventually they get suspended. When a student receives several referrals, or is involved in a fight and sent to an alternative school, the underlying issues still exist, now just at a different school. The student may self-medicate with marijuana before school to help ease his or her mind. Then, when they arrive to school, an administrator smells the weed and searches the student and before the end of the day the kid is at The Detention Center. This is an unending cycle because no one ever takes the time to get to the source of the problem.

In my tenure, I have witnessed young people get arrested for crimes as petty as shoplifting to crimes as serious as first-degree murder. I witnessed young people literally spiral downward after a life-changing event, such as a parent dying or being sent to jail. I have had the unfortunate experience of attending the funeral service of one of my favorite students, Anthony Ray. I have visited the hospital room of a mother whose son was the target of a shooting, but she ended up being shot and having her arm amputated as a result. I have sat in the courtroom and witnessed, time and time again, harsh sentences assigned to young people.

About seven years ago, I wanted to make a profound impact on the young people in my community. So, in 2013, I started volunteering at the Duval Regional Detention Center in Jacksonville, Florida. It was just me with no plan, no curriculum, and honestly, no idea what I was going to do once inside. The only thing I knew for sure was that I wanted to somehow stop young people from making decisions that led them to prison.

Every Tuesday, when I press the buzzer to be let in and an officer answers, I say "I'm here for the girls."

I'll be honest, when I signed up, I wanted to work with the boys; girls never crossed my mind. After I completed all of the necessary paperwork, background checks, and fingerprinting, I was ready. I was extremely devastated when I was told I would be a good fit to work with the girls. In my experience working with children, boys are just easier to deal with. Girls have attitudes, raging hormones, and are just wired differently. I know you're reading this thinking, *You're a girl too*, but trying to get through to a room full of girls is not an easy task.

During my first visit, I went in and introduced myself and I talked mostly about my experiences, just telling them what I thought they needed to hear. I walked away thinking I didn't do or say enough; I couldn't tell if they cared or learned anything. Let's fast forward—seven years later—I am so in love with the girls! Detention Center Tuesday is the one thing in my life that I am consistent with. Every week, I get to tell little girls that they are beautiful, smart, and talented beyond measure. We talk about boys, health, learning how to control anger, how to avoid conflict and most importantly: self-love.

I teach my girls that most of what they are looking for is within, and if they dig deep enough, they will find it.

It has been quite a journey of me meeting girls, some for the first and last time and others repeatedly because it's a revolving door. The Detention Center is simply a holding place until the children are released, direct filed, and charged as an adult or sent to a commitment program. What do you think happens if you take a child from a broken or toxic environment, put them in a cage for a few days, then release them back into broken toxicity? The answer is simple: they will continue to find things that they believe will heal their brokenness. Sometimes this includes drugs, sex, or other poor choices, especially negative associations.

I don't know all of the answers, but I do know that love is a major solution to a lot of the problems young people face. Not love in the intimate sense, but agape love. Martin Luther King Jr. described this love as "unwavering, no matter the circumstance." Love kills jealousy, hate, self-doubt and insecurities. If everyone loved themselves, we wouldn't have time to hate others.

In my own journey from childhood to adulthood to womanhood, I have experienced so much. Most vital to who I am was the absence of both of my natural parents in my upbringing. My mother was seventeen when she birthed me and my grandmother thought it was best to raise me because my mother was too young. My father was never consistently present. He would visit sporadically, send money, and buy gifts on special occasions. On the flip side of things, I was raised in a two-parent home with my grandmother, Rebecca, and my grandfather, David. They have shown me unconditional love and throughout my life attempted to overcompensate in the absence of my parents. I admittedly had voids and my grandparents did their best filling them, but they were still there.

All children need their parents and girls, especially, need their fathers. When we lack a relationship with either of these roles, it is easy to be vulnerable. In adolescence, our interests peak and we become attracted to the opposite sex. It is said that we choose mates similar to our fathers. What about the girls who have no father or anyone filling that role? They are left to figure it out all on their own. Some of us have never been loved properly and never been shown how to love others. While some of us have lived in abnormal, dysfunctional environments that when presented with healthy, normal relationships with the opposite sex, we don't know what to do. Finally, some of us just want love and will accept it in any form, be it normal or abnormal. We put up with poor treatment, various types of abuse, infidelity and we confuse it with love because we simply don't know any better.

Growing up with my grandfather, he always hugged me, told me how pretty I was, supported me in my endeavors and was the first man to tell me he loved me. He still does today. When I need anything, no matter how big or small, he is there to provide it. However, there were times when I called my own father and he didn't answer, or I would invite him to school events and he would tell me he would be there and never showed up.

When we did talk on the phone, he always would say, "You know Daddy loves you." This confused me because *If you love me then why aren't you here*? *Why don't you answer*? *Why do I constantly have to remind you of my existence*? This went on for years until, one day, I was just over it.

When I graduated high school, I was seventeen and pregnant. I mailed him an invite and he said he would be there. I remember calling him the week before and even the day of. After I took my walk across the stage, I looked everywhere; I even waited outside. He was not there! I was so angry and so hurt. Up until that point, it was the biggest moment of my life. Since then, I have had several big moments and he has missed them all, even when I set my pride aside and invited him. The older I get, the less it affects me, but it still isn't a good feeling.

Although I have never been involved with the criminal justice system, I see just how easy it is to become negatively influenced by the opposite sex in exchange for the idea of being loved. In all of my dating experiences, I have always courted men of the streets. I didn't necessarily seek them out; they were attracted to me. I have had my fair share of court dates, jail visits between the glass and prison visitation rooms. When you are young, naïve and in love, you don't see the warning signs of destruction. You only know what feels good in the moment. There were times in my youth when I was asked to do illegal favors, such as drop money off, rent vehicles or simply ride along. All of these things could have been potentially damaging to my future.

There is no positive outcome to the street life for anyone involved. Men prey on the vulnerability of good girls who can help further their agenda. All the while, they have two or three other women in the background fulfilling whatever role you can't.

When I write about this topic, it comes from years of knowledge and my own imperfections. I am not proud of these mistakes, which is why I never speak on them; however, I would be remiss if I led girls into believing that I have not been where they are.

I see girls every week love-smitten by boys who they believe love them back. They will do almost anything to feel wanted and accepted by a male, even if it means losing their freedom. They will do anything to talk to or write them while they are incarcerated. They will plan a pregnancy in the hopes that the boy will hang around. Some, unfortunately, find themselves in situations that land them in prison. I'm not saying fathers are the sole reason for women being incarcerated; however, in addition to other variances, they play a major role. Imagine a world where we all knew love and how to appropriately reciprocate it.

Within these pages, you will read the stories of young ladies and women who, in the absence of their fathers or in unhealthy relationships with men, ended up in some unfortunate circumstances that led to their incarceration. They are baring their souls on these pages in an effort to deter other young girls from making the same mistakes. I want girls everywhere to know you are not alone. I want every girl and woman in prison facilities all over the world to know that you have a voice out here, in me. Finally, to every woman who was able to leave the belly of the beast, you have the responsibility to reach back and encourage someone left behind those fences.

P.S. NEVER GIVE UP HOPE!

I'm Here For The Girls,

The Hope Dealer

Chapter 1: Shara

A Day in The Life of Shara Cooper

"No one went past the surface to really see a day in the life of that eighteen-year-old girl."

I feel like every person within this project is God sent. I either reached out to them because I have seen them on the news, or because someone suggested I reach out to them. If my memory serves me correctly, I was searching for someone else on the Department of Corrections website and Shara came up in my search results. I saw that she was sentenced to life and I saw how young she was—at the time 26—so I decided, in that moment, I would reach out.

I wrote her and she replied. In my second letter I explained that I was writing a book about incarcerated women and wanted to discuss how men played a vital role in it. During this time, I only knew that she was charged with murder, but didn't know any of the details surrounding her case. We corresponded for several months before I traveled to the Florida Women's Reception Center to meet her. We met in 2013. Let's just say, before I left Shara was consoling me—an all too familiar ending with these interviews.

Although I started this process of gathering information and researching well over five years ago, I am not writing consistently. This is not just a "project" for me. I like to get to know the subjects of my writings and aid them in their relief efforts, if possible. Corresponding with women has been difficult because I feel their pain emotionally. I empathize with them on a deep level because I see bits and pieces of myself in each one of them. Shara has been very helpful to me in my own personal struggles by keeping me encouraged and reminding me often of God's promises and his grace. The first letter I ever received from her, I knew she would be someone special in my life for years to come. I consider her a friend.

November 21, 2013

I've been incarcerated now for 7 years and 8 months, away from my family whom I cherish dearly. I'm the baby of four. My mom has two girls and two boys. Originally, I was born in Freeport, Bahamas. I have been living in the States since the age of 3. I came to live with my aunt (my mother's oldest sister) in Miami, Florida. My aunt was unable to have any children. She took very good care of me. We eventually moved to Pompano Beach [when I was about 7] but at the age of 10 I moved to West Palm Beach with my mom because my aunt had lost her job as a nurse and her health began to deteriorate shortly thereafter. Living with my mom was not a bad thing. It's just I had to share with the other children and I wasn't financially spoiled anymore. I love my mom and she did the best that she could do. She is a strong strong woman. My mother got married to my stepfather around the time that I moved there. He is a wonderful country man and they are still together to this day. He is who I consider my father. My stepdad is all that I need.

At the age of 12, I began running away from home. I ran away on two different occasions. The first time, I got into a really bad car accident after a long high-speed chase. My family was looking for me, but I was in a totally different state: South Carolina. They drove all the way there to pick me up. The second time, I was raped. After the guy left, I was in the house alone. I picked up the phone and called home. Again, they came to pick me up. That was enough for me to straighten up and go back home. I learned my lesson and never attempted [to run away] again.

From that point forward, I struggled to live my life right. I say struggled because I didn't have any answers and was trying to find my way with little guidance. That's why I ran away from home. I thought they didn't love me and I was looking for love. I stayed gone about 3-to-4 months, each time of course it was with a boy and I thought he loved me. Silly me! In my family, there is a lack of communication. This greatly affected my personal life and mental stability. I didn't feel like I could talk to my mother. We didn't deal with issues and problems by communicating. She fussed, and we'd just go on as if nothing ever happened. Therefore, I pinned up a lot within. Depression is real. It is a chemical imbalance and many people suffer from it. I have been clinically diagnosed with it since I have been incarcerated. I don't know why I was depressed; I would say that I suffered from age 14 forward. I know now why I cried so much, why I was so sad, why I thought life was useless and why I wanted to kill myself. Now I know it was all depression. I speak on it boldly now, but I haven't always been so strong.

I have two little girls that I love dearly. I had my oldest, "K", at the age of 14. I was young but I took that responsibility like an adult. In all honesty, I had gotten saved and decided to stop having sex with my boyfriend and we did. I was serious about God then. Two months later, I found out I was pregnant. Although very young, I refused to have an abortion and still don't regret that decision. It was the beginning of my 9th grade year. I was elated because I had something that was mine that I could love, that would love me. I knew I was young, but I felt like I was ready, willing and able. I didn't know how, but I knew I could do it.

I learned early on in life about bills, cooking, cleaning and responsibilities. My aunt played a big role in all of that. My teenage years consisted of me always participating in church, work and school. I was in church daily, involved in every function. I got my first unofficial job at 15 working from home for Cintas sorting boxes of emblems. I was a single, young mom so I desperately needed some sort of job to care for my daughter. Two weeks after, I turned 16 and got my first real job at Walgreens. I stayed focused on completing high school with hopes to go to college thereafter. If you would have seen me, it would have appeared that I had my head on straight and everything together. When truly on the inside, I was lost and trying to fill a void.

I realize now that I was attracted to older guys only because I was longing for security and affirmation from a man. All along it was my biological father I needed the most. I hated to admit that I needed him more than I showed. If only I had his voice in my life to tell me about boys. To teach me about my identity. To share with me values. To simply say to me, "I love you". Four separate times, my father rejected me. If only he knew how desperate I was for his attention and affection. So much so that I subconsciously was seeking to replace him at a very early age. I admit I appeared to be okay, but within I was struggling with feeling lost in emotions, desperate for directions and longing for love. Above all, I was crippled in my voice—not knowing how to express myself or who to express myself to. I never knew how to communicate; no one taught me. So when I got into trouble, everyone expected me to talk when I really did not know how to. Fear controlled my voice, while depression controlled my mind. A little girl within, regardless of what the age said, regardless of what the body looked like. A little girl surrounded by many people and many things, yet feeling all alone and lost, not knowing where to begin.

In July of 2005, Shara's boyfriend and the father of her second baby was found murdered in the apartment they shared together. Shara attended the funeral service and after eight months was charged with the murder. Three weeks after his death, she gave birth to their baby girl then lost custody while fighting her case. During the eight months prior to her arrest,

Shara lived with serious depression and was prescribed Prozac along with some other medications, and contemplated sleeping life away. She immediately became a suspect and felt as though the whole world blamed her for his death. After leaving the mental hospital and moving back home with her parents, Shara only had the clothes on her back. The Red Cross gifted her with $500.00 for herself and the children and her parents helped, as well.

After her boyfriend's death, it was difficult trying to live as normal as possible, going through the motions working, attending church and school. There was little contact with Sam's mother. Shara assumed she hated her, however, his mom was welcome to visit her newborn grandbaby whenever she desired. Shara visited her lost love's grave almost every day and would sit there and weep. Within those eight months, investigators continuously came to her parents' house to interview her and even had a warrant to search. After finally being arrested, Shara awaited trial at the Palm Beach County Jail for 22 months before trial. She wrote:

I am in prison today and sitting on a life sentence as a result of his death. I was found guilty of murdering him, setting my home on fire, stealing his truck and stealing his gun. The jury convicted me basically off of this map that the state created labeled "A Day in the Life of Shara Cooper." They used cell phone towers in their attempts to pinpoint me at certain locations. I had trial for 10 days. The last three of those days the jury spent deliberating. They came [back with] the verdict on a Friday. While the foreperson was reading the verdict of guilty, one of the jury members was boo-hoo crying right along with me. I remember seeing her face as if she didn't want that to be her verdict. I went to trial with first-degree murder, but they found me guilty of second-degree murder. My sentencing was delayed three weeks. I was found guilty on February 29th and sentenced on March 25th, 2008.

In September of 2010, my direct appeal was denied with opinion and boy my world came crashing down because I had so much hope in that. I was working in the law library by the time I got the denial, however, I was new to learning the law. I studied and learned that before I can file a 3.850 (motion for post conviction relief), I could file a writ of habeas corpus alleging ineffective assistance of counsel. I filed that in November of 2011 and in March 2012, the fourth district court of appeals reversed my murder conviction for a new trial. They did not overturn the arson charges, which I was aware of that possibility, so I was working on my 3.850 in the meantime.

When I got to prison, I was too nice. I didn't realize that people would be your friend for money. It didn't matter if it was $20 or $200. So I was feeding "friends" not even realizing the games. I trusted these clowns too easily and my feelings continuously got hurt as I continued to get used in one way or another. 99% of girls/women who come to prison fall into a relationship with a woman. Why? Because they/we all want to feel like we have something to connect to. We are lonely and we are trying to fill empty voids in our hearts. We are trying to fit in. So many different reasons, and they are all the wrong reasons. 100% of us women/girls are broken within ourselves and we yearn for another to love us. I have been in relationships consecutively since the age of 13! I'm disgusted just thinking about it. I have always had this deep need to be loved by somebody. That is the main reason I was adamant about keeping my baby at the age of 14. Yet, even after having her and that love, it still wasn't enough. I wanted someone to love me and take care of me, so I continued to yearn to be loved. I neglected Shara and focused hard on pleasing others to hopefully feel loved. Now here I am, years later, realizing I have truly been searching for love in the wrong direction. I have been looking down when I should have been looking up. I realize now that no man, no woman, and no child can fill this void; only God can. Sometimes it's so hard to allow God to fill *that spot because I want something I can see, something I can touch. Faith isn't always so easy. Having two kids, two nieces and a nephew and not watching them go through their phases has been the heartbreak of it all. I die all over again when I think about missing out on them. The kids have always been my weakness—wondering if they are going to hate me and wondering will I see them again or if they will remember me. That is a pain I can't explain and I'm not quite sure there is a cure for it.*

In the midst of it all, I try to stay grounded in the church/chapel. I started praise dancing my second year in. It has been a blessing. There were times when I couldn't pray but I felt like I could meet Him through dance. Honestly, I had let go of God. But God did not let go of me. Even in my deepest, darkest hours—and there were many—something in the depth of my stomach was churning within. I know now that it was God. He wouldn't let me go! Today, I can say that it is all because of Him that I am still standing. I'm still strong. I still have faith and I still have hope. The smile is sincere. My heart is at rest. Don't get me wrong, there are still a few issues that need to be worked on. Renata, I used to be so focused on what I wanted, I wasn't focused on what He wants for me. I just want to please Him with my life, whether it is in here or out there. I want to please God with my life. All my life I was hell-bent on pleasing myself and pleasing people (even at home), but I now know that I never really gave it all over to Him. I never trusted God with my everything. It's all about Him now. My life story is not a story without God in it!

Today, Shara is still fighting for her freedom and currently back in the Palm Beach County jail.

Chapter 2: Nisey

Live Through it and Grow in the Midst of it

*"I always wondered how a loving God could allow
something so tragic to happen in my life."*

It was 2010, after I graduated from Jacksonville University, when I began an internship with the law firm Finnell, McGuinness, Nezami & Andux PA. I spent virtually every Saturday with Mr. Patrick McGuinness working on various tasks. One of my favorite tasks alongside him was jail interviews, where I would go with him to the jail and interview defendants to obtain their side of the story. On this particular Saturday, he told me that he'd received a court-appointed manslaughter case and the defendant was an eighteen-year-old Black female. I went in his office and read through the State's discovery and, quickly, my heart went out to her.

Mr. McGuinness mostly handled homicide and shooting cases. Almost all of the people whom he represented were facing very serious charges and lengthy prison sentences. It was rare to come across a manslaughter where two young people were mishandling a firearm and one of them ended up dead.

We walked to the jail from the office on Bay Street, signed in at the desk and boarded the elevator to the third floor where women are housed. I am always nervous on initial visits because here I am, a perfect stranger asking someone in jail to talk about a moment in time I'm sure they want to forget. Nisey entered the interview room and sat in the middle of Mr. McGuinness and I. She was quiet and timid. I, at the time, was 24. I didn't say much, but my mind was racing and I wanted to ask many questions.

I wanted to know what happened; not with the case but in her life. What led her to this point? I am of the belief that to every story there is a backstory and the backstory will answer every question. I never got to ask my questions, but I learned at the sentencing hearing, where Nisey was given 15 years, that she had been sexually molested by her own father. *How does a girl have a positive relationship with men once the man who is supposed to love her most violates her?*

In a letter dated January 2015, Nisey wrote: *I am so thankful that you found it in your heart to write me again. I am so sorry for not writing you back the first time. Please accept my apology. You are one of the only people I've heard from after my case other than my family. No one reached out to me. Everyone pretty much gave up on me and you know, Ms. Renata, I gave up hope. I felt like my life was not even worth it anymore. I didn't know how to deal with the pain on the inside. I became involved with the homosexual lifestyle [because] I wanted to belong to anything that would fill up the emptiness I felt on the inside.*

I was born July of 1991 in Haiti. I lived with my grandparents from the time I was one-year old until I was eight years old. My mother was living in Port-Au-Prince. My father's parents did not approve of her, so she left me with them and moved to Port-Au-Prince to make a living for herself. My mother's parents were very poor. My father was in the U.S. before I was born, so I did not meet him until I was eight years old. He brought me a lot of gifts and made sure I had the best of everything. My grandparents were farmers and used to take me everywhere with them. They used to take me out with them every time they did cultivation. I used to feed the chickens and they taught me how to plant seeds for harvest. A lot of the kids my age were playing with Barbie dolls. I was playing with marbles, jumping rope with other kids, learning how to milk cows and grow crops. We did not have a refrigerator. I didn't even know what that was until I turned eight and moved to Port-Au-Prince with my mother. We had one little small TV. My uncle used a solar system to make it work and when it did, it only had one channel. We did not have electricity so we used lamps and candles.

At seven years old, I was raped by my older cousin. He told me to not say anything. I never did until now. My mother doesn't even know this. Other than that, I can remember being very happy. I was free-spirited. My grandparents forbade me and my cousins from other people's houses or to pick up anything from the floor because they did not want any harm to come to us. The people in the village practice a lot of witchcraft so my grandparents always wanted us to be careful and safe.

My father eventually made arrangements with my mother for me to move with her. He rented a house and my mother moved in; she made a trip back to come get me. I went to a Catholic school and was very much sheltered. I was an in-house girl. I did not have any friends. I only played with my cousin. I had my first birthday party at the age of 10.

I learned how to speak English in the seventh grade at the New American School. It was very hard for me because I didn't know how to adjust. I was scared a lot. The pressure of trying to be somebody else made me feel inferior and the boys used to make fun of me. One of them pretended to like me and was making me do things I did not know at the time were not right. I wanted to fit in with all the other kids. Most of them were teenagers that were sent to Haiti by their parents. Some of them were troubled teenagers that the state kicked out of the country, so I was exposed to some behaviors that I knew nothing about. I was only 12 years old so I was very curious about everything.

The school was very big. It started from first to twelfth grade and was a lot of pressure for me. I wanted to fit in, so it didn't matter what the older kids had me do. Then in 2005, the month of March, I moved to the United States. I finished my eighth grade year at Crystal Lake Middle School where we lived in Pompano. The week before my 9th grade year in 2005, that's when my nightmare began. I was being sexually molested by my father. My mother knew there was something going on because my father would come home real late. He lied to my mom but she never knew that my father was coming into my bedroom every night. He'd try to manipulate me into having sex with him, but deep down I knew it was not the right thing to do so I told him no every time. Sometimes he would try and force himself on me. I would kick and try to fight him. We moved to Tampa in the month of October. I was attending King High School and things got worse. By this time, my mother was six months pregnant with my little sister. My father continued to force himself on me, but I fought him every time. He became very abusive towards me physically. One night, my mother heard a commotion in my room. I ran out of the room and went to the bathroom. My father was still in my bedroom when my mother came out and I told her that my father was hiding in the closet in my bedroom. My mother was hurt but she believed my dad when he said he didn't know what was wrong with him but he'll stop. My mother asked me had he ever actually had sex with me. I told her no but that he tried many times. Well, that was that and nothing changed. If anything, it got worse.

The physical abuse was too much for me to even bear. So I went to school one day and I told one of my teachers. I was so scared. I used to dread going back home because of everything that was going on. We ended up going back to Haiti after the police came and questioned my dad. I don't know what they told him, but they left. He almost killed me that day. When he said we were going back to Haiti, I knew he was going to kill me and I did not want to go back. I told him I'm not going because of fear. I knew he could kill me if he wanted to when we got to Haiti. He forced me to get in the car and if

I didn't, he said he would kill me. I got in the car and we stopped at my uncle's house in Ft. Lauderdale. My dad came up with this lie that we had to tell my uncle once we got to his house. We left early the next day for the airport. The whole time I was on the airplane I knew my life was over.

When we got to Haiti, I was the villain; everybody was mad at me. They told my dad to kill me if I'm going to bring shame to the family, but nobody really knew what happened. My mother stayed in Fort Lauderdale with my uncle to have my sister. My father went a month without speaking to me, then one day he just lost it and almost killed me. I went a few weeks with my body hurting because he used an extension cord. I was bleeding everywhere he punched and kicked me. After those weeks, he started being nice to me again. Then he started coming in my room again a lot of nights. I used to try and sleep with my little brother right under me because he brought me so much comfort. I felt that if he was there my dad would not try to harm me. It worked for a couple days, then he told me he didn't want him sleeping in my room anymore. He was three years old then. I was so afraid to sleep by myself that I started sleeping on the floor in my cousin's bedroom. Even this did not stop my dad. He would come and get me in the middle of the night and tell me that my brother needed changing, but in reality he was coming on to me. He pulled out a gun one time and told me if I did not have sex with him he was going to kill me. I told him I would rather die. I was able to call my mom and ended up coming back to the U.S. in the beginning of 2006.

Once I came back in 2006, we lived in Fort Lauderdale and I attended North East High. I was still having problems socializing with others. At home, my crisis began; my dad was coming in my bedroom touching me. I didn't know he was watching me in the bathroom while I was taking showers. How I found out was when he had me in his car one night, he asked me who I was talking to in the bathroom. I had a habit of talking to myself while I looked in the mirror. I was embarrassed at first that he caught me having a full conversation with myself, then it dawned on me: How many times was he actually watching me through the window? Did he somehow purposely move the blinds? All of these questions were running through my head. Every time I was going in to take a shower, I double checked the blinds and my paranoia began. I started having the feeling that I was being watched everywhere I went. The atmosphere at home was often hostile. My little sister and brother were my lifeline. They were young and did not understand anything that was taking place. I lost myself in playing with them. They brought me so much joy and I know they genuinely loved me.

After a few months, we moved to Jacksonville, Florida, and my father was disappointed in me because I had to repeat the 9th grade. I didn't know what he expected when I had to go to four different high schools my freshman year. I started attending Sandalwood High and I really loved that school. My grades were great. My father went months without bothering me, so in my mind that was great too. I believed him and my mom worked out a situation for us because they would leave the house at 6PM for work and come back early before I went to school. I didn't know much about the arrangement, however, it worked in my favor... I thought.

One particular night I was sleeping and I locked the doors to my room, which I was not allowed to do. I felt someone trying to pull my pajamas down and I woke up screaming and shaking; my window was left half open. My mother came running and my dad was in the closet. I would not stop crying and I don't believe my mother knew how to comfort me. She was arguing with my dad and it was almost time for me to get ready for school. I was shocked, hurt and devastated.

I don't recall who introduced me to MySpace. I started getting involved on that website and I became addicted. It was my only escape from my reality. It was a place I could pretend to be someone else. On Myspace, I had friends. In the real world, I didn't have any. Social media became my biggest influence. My grades started dropping because I was staying up late and sleeping during class hours. My reality was not my reality anymore. I was being pulled deeper and deeper into the unknown. I met this guy on Myspace. I did not know his real name, his age or his background. Once I started talking to him, days after we decided to meet. He asked me where I lived and I told him. He asked me when my parents were going to be gone and I told him. He gave me his phone number to call him once they were gone. That night, I did. He told me he was on his way. In order to find the courage to meet him, I had to tell myself it was not Nisey the scary, timid, naïve little girl who was going to meet him. It was Lil Haiti, the bitter, angry and bold young woman I had become.

I went to call him back and he told me he was outside. Once I got outside, he asked me to get in his car; I did. He never once asked me how I'm doing. Nothing. He just wanted to make out and have sex. Now talking of sex, I was not actually a virgin, because my father confessed to me that he only wanted to be the one to take my virginity. When I went back to Haiti in 2005, I was all game for the first guy that wanted to have sex with me. In my mind I felt like I had one over on my dad. Just in case it got to a place that I could not defend myself. I just did not want him to be the first man I had sex with.

Here I am in a car with a stranger, who wants to have sex and I'm afraid because I don't want to. Then I'm scared if I don't, he would rape me, so I gave it up willingly. In truth, it was unwillingly because I didn't want to be there. I didn't realize that this experience was going to become a constant cycle in my life.

One morning, I woke up with my father's fist and shoes on my face and body. I didn't know what I'd done to set him off. He threw the phone at me and told me to call the number back that just called early that morning. Apparently, whoever called hung up when it was answered. I called back and no one picked up. Somehow, he was able to hack into my MySpace account and found out that I was living a pretend life. I don't know where my father's anger came from, however, when he called me close to him to read some of the lies and some truths I fabricated on the internet, he punched and kicked me like I was a stranger (which we were). I learned that you could live in a house for years with someone and not really know them.

The next day I went to school and my arms and legs were still bruised from the extension cord. It was 90-something degrees and I was wearing a jacket. My eye still had the blood spot from my dad's fist. Once in school, I started to plan on how I was going to run away because I did not want to go home. I was scared my dad was going to lose it one day and kill me and I was also scared that he might end up raping me, then I'll get pregnant. I was terrified to go back home. I wanted to run away, but I didn't know where to go. I didn't have any friends and I didn't know anyone. I decided to talk to my history teacher. He took me to the administration office. They asked me various questions about my life at home and asked me to take off my jacket. They sent me home and told me DCF was going to see me. Once I got home, I acted like nothing ever happened.

I went to get my brother from school. When I got back, my dad came and dragged me from the chair. He grabbed the chair and I rolled over before it could hit me. I laid in the fetal position with my hand over my ear and my elbows covering my face. The whole time my father was kicking and punching me. In that moment, I wanted to die; I did not want to live. What hurt me was hearing my four-year-old little brother screaming and crying for my dad to stop while my mom was sitting on the couch watching everything. Eventually my dad stopped. He called the police to come get me. One officer took me in my room and checked me. My father was arrested and I went to Y.C.C. (Youth Crisis Center).

The few months I stayed in YCC, I didn't know if I was coming or going. I told them that I didn't want to go back to my parents' house and my dad didn't want me to come back because he didn't want me to corrupt my siblings. I went to my first foster home on the Eastside ran by an older woman. She had other foster kids also. In the pursuit of me trying to find myself, happiness and love, I became a prostitute, which at the time I didn't know nor understand. The men lied to me; they told me they cared and even used the word love just to get me to have sex. It seemed like I was doing it willingly, however, every single time I laid up with one of those men I felt more empty because I was unwillingly having sex with them.

One of the foster girls who knew I was having sex told me, "Nothing in the world is free." She told me if I was going to have sex to make them pay. I started trying different drugs that the foster girls were bringing in and they were teaching me how to prostitute. One particular day, the grandson of my foster parent and his girlfriend came to pick me and another foster girl up to go see their apartment. In the middle of the night, the grandson woke me up and told me it was his birthday and asked me what I was going to give him.

I did not understand what he was saying so I replied, "I don't know, what do you want?" He started telling me he wanted me, so on and so forth. I got up then we walked to his bathroom. Well, his girlfriend who was pregnant at the time caught us and she tried to fight me. I was still oblivious to what I did wrong. She kicked us out and on the silent car ride home, I felt like a person with no soul. No direction. We went to his friend's house for the remainder of the night. Once we got back to my foster house, all hell broke loose. I doubt they reported it because he was over 18. They all kept it hush hush and I did too. Nobody asked and I never told. I can't recall the events that transpired for me to get moved out of that foster home. I transferred from Andrew Jackson High to Raines High School. I hated that foster care; everything was locked and her kids were mean to me. I then went to a group home called Pearl Cottage and started attending Robert E. Lee High School. I have vague memories of that high school. The group home was my safe haven. The staff was good to me, however, I was not good to myself. I started skipping classes with the other foster kids; they were my influence. I didn't know who I was and I was lost. I looked for validation in everyone and everything else.

In November 2007, the state decided to send me back to my parents. I was having supervised visits with my parents and they had to take classes. Once I moved back, I started attending Terry Parker. My mother introduced me to Jehovah Witnesses; we were going to the Kingdom Hall for weeks and my father had not spoken to me. I did my best to stay out of his way. At Terry Parker, instead of skipping school I was skipping class. I had my own inner demons I was struggling with and school was the last place I wanted to be. I could not focus. I was living recklessly and didn't care if I lived or died. I did not want to be on planet earth.

Nisey and her father continued to be at odds with one another. The abuse progressed to fighting each other. DCF finally removed her from the home in 2008 and she switched schools yet again and was placed back into foster care. At her new foster home, Nisey was treated like family. Her foster parents' grandson came over one day and they had sex. They never mentioned it to anyone. Nisey had learned to numb herself and not have feelings toward these incidents.

"During my stay, every night I would ask myself who am I? Where do I come from? What am I here for?"

At 17, her life was spiraling out of control, dating a 40-year-old man, maintaining an on-and-off relationship. It was also during this time that she began to date girls. Once Nisey turned 18, she received independent living and moved into an apartment, then dropped out of high school to later attend community college where she met some girls who were popular and cool. This intrigued Nisey, who wanted to be popular and cool, too. Her best friend at the time was kicked out of her home with her mother, so Nisey offered her a place to stay. On November 30, 2009 another friend asked her if her boyfriend could come over and Nisey agreed. About a half hour later, he arrived with two other friends with weed and liquor. One of the guys had a gun with him so they started taking pictures with the gun. Nisey knew two of the guys, but did not know one of them; his name was Emmanuel. They were all drinking and having fun. After a few hours they became hungry and decided to go to McDonald's. When they got in the car, it wouldn't rev up, but once they finally got it started, the gas light was on. This should have been a sign but it wasn't and they proceeded to drive to the gas station.

Once they arrived to the gas station, Emmanuel went in but it was closed. He walked back out to the car as Nisey sat in the back seat playing with the gun and dancing to the music. Emmanuel leaned in the car and unbeknownst to Nisey, there was a bullet in the chamber; the gun went off. Everyone inside the vehicle ducked down thinking someone was shooting at them. The victim's best friend was also in the backseat. He opened the car door and Emmanuel was on the ground shot dead. They called the police. Upon arrival, Nisey was arrested and charged with manslaughter. She could not believe what happened and didn't even know his name until after the shooting.

Once in jail, depression set in. Nisey went weeks without eating and questioning how this could happen to someone with such a promising life and not her who didn't want to live. It took her years to forgive herself. In 2012, while sitting in confinement, she was fed up and sick and tired. After crying out to God and asking Him to heal her and change her heart, she dedicated her life to Christ.

I've prayed often for my victim's family that they would forgive me. I can say that I am at peace with myself and God. I am still learning how to accept His will and His ways. To anybody reading my story, I can tell you that this is just the beginning. As long as I am still alive, my story will be continued. We all have gone through some scary experiences and devastating moments. I am reminding you that there is hope for you. The storms in your life did not come to take you out. How many times have you experienced a storm in your life and you did not believe you were going to survive? Whether it was financial or a relationship, you held on to the hope that it will get better. You are stronger and wiser than before.

When Ms. Renata met me, I was timid, lost, angry and bitter. I hated myself, the world and everybody in it. Now for all the glory of God I am wiser, better, stronger and more powerful than I ever thought I'd be. My goal when I get out is to be a motivational speaker to give back and make a difference in someone's world. I want to continue what I'm doing here out there. We can all inspire one another and encourage and build each other up. If I survived through the storms, you can too. There is hope for you. I would like to thank you, Ms. Renata, for being the vessel that God can use to make all of this possible. May God bless you indeed and continue to enlarge your territory.

Chapter 3: Roteia

Don't Judge My Book by Its Cover

"I started getting in trouble around age 14
so I could go live with my momma…"

Until the age of two, Roteia lived with her mom, Rhonda, and afterwards was raised by her grandmother, who sheltered her as a child. Throughout her childhood Roteia would often see her mom and longed to live with her. However, Roteia's mom was a young nineteen-year-old mother and unstable. At 22, she got into trouble and ended up serving three years in prison.

Roteia would purposely get into trouble hoping that her grandmother would send her to live with her mother. At age 15, in the 9th grade, she met Tony and her wish came true; she moved back in with her mom.

Roteia didn't like Tony at first but he liked her so much he just grew on her. Tony left Jacksonville and moved to Georgia when they were 16. At 17, he was back in Jacksonville and was locked up in the county jail. The entire time he was in jail, they stayed in touch and she visited. By the time Tony was released, Roteia had turned 18. On the day of Tony's release, Roteia and her mom went to pick him up and he stayed at their house that night, April of 2013. The two were inseparable and spent every day together. Tony was on probation and trying to stay out of trouble. Before long, he was hanging out with friends who were a negative influence.

On August 6, 2013, according to news reports, there were four suspects on a random hunt looking for a victim to rob. The news reports also stated that when the victim was approached he reached for a knife and was subsequently shot. It was never determined who fired the actual shot that killed the victim.

The three stories of the participants were conflicting at trial and it was left up to the jury to determine, based on the evidence presented, who was responsible for the tragic shot. Roteia was a willing participant and driver of the getaway car.

While sitting in the car waiting on her three co-defendants, Roteia heard two gunshots ring out. After the shooting, the three young men, Tony, Josh and J.D., ran back to the car hysterical and in a panic. Once in the car, J.D. couldn't find his I.D. He called his girlfriend and asked if it was at her house and she said *No*. They went and looked at Roteia's house and it wasn't there either. He had in fact dropped his I.D. at the crime scene. About two to three days after the incident, J.D. was picked up for questioning and they hadn't heard from him. Roteia looked him up online and that confirmed he had been arrested for murder.

J.D.'s arrest made the others paranoid. In their teenaged minds, they were going to run to avoid being questioned. This made Roteia extremely nervous. She called her sister and they went to grab a bite to eat. Before Roteia could even bite into her food, ten police officers arrived to arrest her. They placed her in handcuffs and took her downtown where she was charged with first-degree murder and attempted armed robbery. Her mother fainted at the Police Memorial Building.

Once booked, Roteia called Tony from the holding cell and said, "It's over, I'm never going home." He started crying hysterically; his mom and sister cried in the background too. The following morning during breakfast, the sight of the food on the tray caused her to tear up. At first appearance, she was officially charged with murder. She called Tony, but his mom answered and told her that he had just been picked up.

Roteia spent the next two years in the county jail. Some days she would break down crying in her bunk: *"In jail your days depend a lot on the people you surround yourself with."*

Roteia would stare at the red light and think to herself, *I will never drive again.* She often wondered if she would ever go home and dealt with the uncertainty of her future while trying to maintain her sanity. There was one officer in particular that was very nasty to her and would shakedown her cell and tear up her personal belongings. Going back and forth was exhausting.

Roteia's first offer from the State was life, then 50 years, then 25, then 10. Her sentencing hearing was very emotional, with her grandmother, mom, uncle and little sister present. Roteia plead out to a sentence of 53 months, but was sentenced to six years. After the sentencing, Roteia didn't want to talk to anyone and felt a sense of relief and was ready to get it over with, but was afraid to go to prison because of the stories she had heard. Throughout this entire ordeal, her mother was very supportive; they wrote each other and she attended court dates. Today, they remain very close.

In less than 30 days after sentencing, Roteia was at Florida Women's Reception Center in Ocala, Florida. She was housed in confinement for three weeks due to being a youthful offender. In confinement, she was only allowed to shower every other day and escorted to shower in shackles. The youthful offender dorm is a boot camp where inmates have to do physical training every day. In prison, Roteia says it is emotionally better than jail. According to her, the inmates were OK; it is the officers that make the prison experience bad. In January 2017, after being in prison for roughly four years, Roteia was selected for the BTU (Basic Training Unit). This rigorous boot camp style program allows participants to go home early and complete their sentence on probation. Looking back, Roteia believes this program was the hardest experience of her life. She had to physically train and work hard to go home. Many inmates begin this program but don't successfully complete it. In July of 2017, Roteia was released from prison. She initially experienced a lot of ups and downs with finding a job and a place to stay because of the label of felon.

Today, Roteia is the mother a one-year-old daughter, gainfully employed and has no regrets about what she went through because she learned a lot being incarcerated. Prison taught her to be humble and to block out negativity. In prison she couldn't allow the environment to overtake her.

Her advice to girls and young women in her shoes is: *"No matter how much you may think you love someone, don't allow him to take you off track because after it's all said and done you have to do the time alone. After the time is over and done, you are the one that has to live as a convicted felon— and when people look at your record, that's all they see."*

During the process of publishing this book, Roteia's first love and co-defendant, Tony, was killed in prison in September of 2020. This chapter is dedicated to him. May his soul rest in peace.

Until you've been arrested
and spent endless days in jail
and walked 100 miles without ever leaving your cell
Until you've faced a judge
and entered your guilty plea
and you've heard the words of judgment
that you won't be going free

Until your days turn into weeks,
weeks turn into months,
and months turn into years
of you shedding endless tears

Until you fight to keep your sanity
and you've gone through all these years
and lost all human will

How can you look at me and say
you know just how I feel?

Through it all, even when they tried to break me,
I made it through every time and still smiled through the
whole four years.

Chapter 4: Emerald

Daddy Loves You

"I'd say the lack of love from my father ignited all of the things in my life. I can't fully blame him, but if he knew how to be a father, I wouldn't be here."

In 2013, I traveled to the Lowell Correctional Institution in Ocala, Florida. The assistant warden at the time advised me that Lowell was the largest facility in the country with nearly 5000 beds. That statistic stuck with me and I began to think to myself, *Surely many of these women are mothers. They are young. They are old. They are me.* I wondered what happened in their lives that led them to prison. Lowell has inmates from juveniles all the way up to death row. Women are thought of as loving, caring nurturers; not labeled as criminals serving harsh time. I wanted to investigate the 'why' to their current circumstance. A co-worker of mine told me about Emerald and I reached out to her. We have stayed in contact ever since.

Emerald was wearing the state-issued blue inmate uniform the first time we met. She waddled out in shackles and handcuffs escorted by an officer. This was very different than the other interviews I had conducted. The guard explained to me that Emerald was in closed management custody and had been for four years. This meant that she was on 23-hour lockdown with few privileges. Although African American, her skin tone was very light as a result of being inside so long with no exposure to sunlight. The whole ordeal was sort of intimidating to meet a young lady charged with murder in chains like an animal.

In our correspondence, prior to meeting, Emerald was very sweet. She wrote poetry, spoke of God and adored her little sister, Christina, although they hadn't spoken in years.

Emerald is hard on the surface but very loveable on the inside. After getting to know her, I now know that the proverbial walls built outside of her are a result of the life she was dealt.

My name is Emerald. I am a 25-year-old woman that was sentenced to 40 years' imprisonment at the age of 15 for second-degree murder and armed robbery in Jacksonville, Florida. Growing up, I had no mother figure; all I had was my dad. I mean, yes, I had aunts, grandmas and even cousins, but I didn't have that nurturing that only a mother can give to her child.

I was born in Atlanta, Georgia, to Claude Barner Jr. & Brenda Steger. Up until the age of six, I lived there with my mom and four siblings. Due to her severe mental problems (my mom was schizophrenic) me and my little sister, Christina, came down to Jacksonville with our dad. I can barely remember my mom. There's things I learned about her through the internet or my legal work. I don't know her voice, barely remember how she looks, etc. I know I love pancakes and bacon because that's all she used to feed us. I remember constantly moving around with her. Although she hasn't been in my life, I LOVE my momma and just want to feel her hold me and tell me why she hasn't been in my life. I want to tell her my fears and pain and be reassured.

Once we moved, it's like I kind of took on the role of mom. I learned how to clean the dishes, swept and mopped the kitchen and so much more. I was still a child and I enjoyed my childhood. I loved school and honestly it was a place to get away. I got in trouble in school because I held a lot of anger inside so when I snapped, it was bad. I got into fights with girls, teachers, and sometimes boys, too. Though I enjoyed my childhood, it was a rough one.

My father had a violent temper. There was the littlest thing that could upset him and instead of talking about it, he lashed out. One time when I was 7 years old, I got a beating because I couldn't write my name how he wrote it. That doesn't mean my dad wasn't a caring father though. There were times I remember him picking me up and hugging me saying, "Daddy loves you!" I won't lie, I was afraid of him; if he yelled at me, I'd get afraid and cry. There's a couple of times he told me he didn't think I was his and my mother should've gotten a DNA test, but other than that, to him I was a big liar and manipulator.

Deep down inside I believed, and still believe, my father hated me. For a while I hated my daddy to a horrible point, but an officer here opened my mind and helped me to work on forgiving him. It was just last year I forgave my dad. At a young age I went looking for attention in the wrong manner. The built-in hurt and anger I took out on others, so I guess you can say at 9 I truly got tired. It was during this time that I was molested by an older family member. I was afraid of my dad and he always called me a liar, so I never told him; I just kept it inside. But I really openly got tired at the age of 13. That was the first time I ran away. If I can remember, I went to this boy's house who had a crush on me. I spent time with his older sister and she did my hair. Later that day, I was walking down the street and my father was driving home and saw me. I saw him and just went home. When I got there, he was waiting with the belt. Despite my dad going to jail for beating me and my older brother and me and Christina going into foster care for about a year, despite more family attempting to help guide me and Christina and show us what family is supposed to be like, nothing changed.

In foster care, I saw how no one really cared; they were just there for the money. When they looked at us foster kids, all they saw was a chore and dollar signs. I had one parent tell me she wanted to keep me and maybe adopt me because I got an SSI check! Some of my foster parents (the husband) started coming on to me until I told, ended up getting in a fight and arrested. Some really didn't care and it's sad.

Once in foster care, I got worse. I ran away from every home. I fought a lot, I started smoking weed and I became sexually active. I had sex with men for multiple reasons, but as I got older I realized that it was mainly for attention and to please them. It was a sick way of having a male figure who approved me, acknowledged me when I did good and paid attention to me since my dad never did.

Honestly, I was confused and lost deep down inside. I had a thing for women undercover but because I feared my dad and I knew he was against the gay lifestyle, I didn't entertain them. Sometimes I sold myself just to have somewhere to lay my head and eat. I would sleep on park benches, at bus stops, at abandoned houses, in hallways of apartments or even on the porch of a house just to rest from walking around all day. I was tired. Every time I would get picked up and taken home, I'd run away again because I refused to be there. I lost my virginity at age 13 to a boy named "D" and in the beginning I would run to him a lot. I thought I was in love but really I didn't know what love was. He and I were like two lost and broken souls together feeding off of one another, while at the same time destroying each other even more. I tried to do right, but one thing after another kept me from staying at home—whether it was a perverted foster parent or me fighting.

Eventually, I ended up living with family and I started doing good. Being with my cousins really helped me. I was almost a kid again, until my uncle by marriage started molesting me. I tried to tell my aunt, but she didn't believe me or my sister. After that, I started lashing out again and fighting everybody. Win, lose, or draw, I fought! I ran away again and things kind of got bad after that. I started messing with an older man who was already in a relationship. I broke in houses, stole from people, fought, smoked weed and was shot at. I found myself in reckless situations. My life was a chaotic hell. I became suicidal. My foster mom was right when she predicted correctly that I would end up somewhere that would force me to change. Since then, I've been through a lot, but I've changed a lot.

In prison I've been sprayed, jumped on by officers, tried to commit suicide so many times. I've lost family members to the grave, boys I used to hang with have died and I have grown. I think of the disregard that I had for human life. Never in the past did I stop to consider them. I was selfish and lost and it has taken for me to come to prison to realize that. I have come to terms with who I am, who I was, what I've done, who I've hurt and what I lost. I can't continuously point the finger because in the end I chose to do the things I did while destroying lives in the process. God saved me; He knew I needed it. I'm not perfect, but I'm not what I used to be.

In 2014, Emerald told me about a letter from her mother. I immediately asked if I could reach out to her. She sent me her mailing address and I wrote her explaining to her I was working on this project. Her mother, Brenda Steger, replied to me and I never shared the details of the letter with Emerald until now. Brenda, who resided in Atlanta, Georgia, passed away two years later.

The letter stated, *"What do I say about 8 lb. 4 oz. beautiful Emerald? She was just that and grew up pleasantly. She was a quiet little girl. She slept most of the time and didn't give me a lot of trouble, but had attention deficit disorder. She would turn around in circles and fall. I would worry that she would hurt herself. My daughter was perfect in my eyes. The Lord blessed me with a wonderful daughter; one I could only tell about. I would tell her how much I loved her, and hugged her and loved her much. I had games I bought from the store and we would play with them. I pray her time in jail will be another overcomer for her. I love Emerald very much. She thinks that because I let her father take her that somehow I didn't love her, which couldn't be farther from the truth. I felt she could do better with him."*

Although Brenda has passed, her short presence in Emerald's life was impactful. Brenda was sure to express her love for Emerald and that she wanted so much more for her life than she could have offered. Emerald continues to reflect on her story, still grieving while incarcerated.

At fourteen, I was arrested for aggravated assault on my sister, fighting, resisting arrest without violence, grand theft auto and then my charges now, in which I received 40 years, all between age 14 and 15. In foster care, I saw how no one really cared; they were just [there] for the money. I was arrested at age 15 on July 7, 2008 for second degree murder and armed robbery. Two detectives pulled me in for questioning and I was arrested immediately. I was in the county for one and a half years. When I was locked up, all I wanted to do was go home. I started regretting a lot. I can't say I was afraid of going to DDC because some group homes are worse. I was afraid of what was going to happen.

When I got to DDC, I began praying and reading my bible and I was stressing really bad and though I didn't know it, I was pregnant and lost my baby. That took a toll on me, but I was thankful that my baby wouldn't have to go through what I went through with DCF. When I was charged as an adult, I was confused. I didn't know what to expect at the county jail. When I got to the county, I got into a fight with another juvenile and caught a battery charge which got dropped later. I was placed on lockdown because of the fight and I started disliking C.O.'s because of it. I mean I already didn't like officers, but that made it worse. I started acting up and cursing a lot of the C.O.'s out. One of the officers clung to me and tried helping me change. At first, of course, I didn't like her. I stayed on lockdown a lot because of my temper; I was always ready to fight.

I got tired of going to court proceedings and at one point just was ready to give up and take a life sentence, but my public defender wouldn't allow it. I ended up getting a new public defender and he wasn't a good one. When the time came for my sentencing, having to sit and listen to everyone make me out to seem like a monster upset me a lot. I testified for myself, the victim's son spoke and so did my detectives. Because I pled guilty, we didn't have to do much. The judge asked the State Attorney for their recommended sentence, which was 40 years and my PD tried to get me 10 years. The judge took the state's recommendation.

I lost all hope. I lost faith in God. I hated the court system. I just developed a nastier attitude than I came to jail with. I cried once and after that I was just rude and nasty.

One C.O. tried to tell me, "You know God has the last word." He was African.

Before he could finish I said, "F a God" and even now I wonder what happened to me?

Since then, I have worked on my relationship with God, but back then—to me—there wasn't one. I couldn't eat or sleep all day the next day; all I could think about was, "Soon as I get to prison I'ma make them kill me"… They gonna have to kill me!

In November of 2019, Emerald was re-sentenced to a term of 30 years in which she will be eligible for a sentencing review and a potential early release. Throughout the years, I have received poetry from Emerald and her words are a perfect expression of how she feels. In the future, she wants to publish her poetry collection.

One of the poems sent to me is titled "Abuse":

The tears won't stop, the beatings won't quit
It's painful to my mind to go through it again
Things that happened to me from the age of six
All began once I felt that dreaded hit
Didn't understand how you could love me but hurt me
I know you've seen the pain I was enduring
No I wasn't perfect, I was only a child sitting in bed
and crying my pain away at night
The more pain I felt was on the inside indeed
The reason I cried was from the hate
not the bruises I seen
It's painful to go back to the times I needed love
Someone to wipe my tears
'cause of the hits that stung.

Chapter 5: Kenitra

Unbroken

*"Justice doesn't mean the bad guys go to jail.
It means that someone pays the price."*

In 2011, I saw the news of a Jacksonville Sheriff's Office employee arrested for leaking confidential information. As someone with familiarity with the criminal justice system, I remember thinking to myself, *He or she will be terminated.* I didn't follow the case and honestly didn't think much of it after the initial news broadcast. Fast forward to several months later—I saw a young lady whose name I recognized, but I didn't personally know her, had been sentenced to 12 years in prison. Almost immediately, my heart ached. I reached out to her cousin, whom I know through a mutual association and asked for details. Surely there had to be more than what the news reported: that she had sent a photograph of undercover police officers to her husband upon his request via email. I told her cousin that I was sorry for what had happened, and I referred her family to a reputable attorney. I was literally in shock at the amount of time she received for sharing confidential information.

Kenitra had worked at the Sheriff's Office for seven years at the time of her arrest. She had only been reprimanded at work once in her tenure there for leave from work. Despite being a married mother of two beautiful children who grew up with a large family in a loving home, she was charged with 14 counts of disclosure or use of confidential criminal justice information (a third-degree felony), three counts of misuse of confidential information (a first-degree misdemeanor), three counts of obstructing justice (a first-degree misdemeanor), and three counts of obstructing justice. Kenitra was sentenced to 11 times more time than the known drug dealer with whom her husband provided the photographs to. Her husband received no time at all.

On June 22, 2011, Kenitra was arrested and booked at the pre-trial detention facility in Jacksonville, Florida. After the detective told her she was being arrested, he allowed her to make a phone call. In her own words:

After being interrogated and told that I was about to be transported to the jail, I called my husband and told him that I was being arrested.

On my way to jail, his response was, "For what I asked you for?" as if he automatically knew what was going on. He also stated, "I'm not going to tell you how high your bond is."

He was somewhat supportive. During that time, I was able to call home, order canteen/commissary and he came to visit me every Sunday. I just felt like it wasn't enough and he could have done more. I felt like he wasn't involved enough with my attorney. Everything was left up to my mom. I started with 33 counts and for each charge the bond was set at $50,000 each, which made my bond $1.3 million, so I was unable to bond out. Before I went to arraignment, 21 of the charges were dropped. It is still unclear to me how they ended up with 12 charges. I went before the judge for a bond reduction, but it was denied because the State continuously claimed they were adding more charges and the judge said it made no sense for me to post bond and be rearrested.

Once I was booked and sent upstairs, there were some ladies waiting to be released and one of them prepared me for what to expect once inside the dorm. She told me that once I walked inside they would scream, "Fresh Meat." It was after 8:30 p.m. when I finally made it inside the dorm, which means they were all locked down in their cells.

When they opened the door to the dorm and the girls saw someone new entering, they surely did begin to scream, "Fresh Meat." Since I was prepared for it, I actually laughed. I went to my assigned cell, #22, upstairs. There was another young lady in there reading a book. I walked in and quietly spoke, then I made my bunk and laid down in an attempt to go to sleep. My cellmate, better known as Bunkie, was really nice. She had already been there for about six months, so she kind of showed me the ropes and told me how things worked.

Seven and a half years later, I still remain in custody of the Dept. of Corrections. My son is now 11 and my daughter is almost 8 years old. Earlier this year, I had to file a motion for enforcement because their father wasn't abiding by the terms of our divorce, which allows me two phone calls a week and frequent visitation. During that time, I went a month without speaking to the children and five months without seeing them. The judge granted me the motion and now I'm talking to them more and working toward more visits.

My son has taken my incarceration very hard. Prior to my arrest, he had no issues. Once this happened, he shut down and had a difficult time understanding why his mom has never returned home. My daughter didn't quite understand why all the other children had their mom and she didn't. We went through a difficult time with her being angry with me and not wanting to talk when I called. This was heartbreaking for me. In this environment, you have no one's shoulder to cry on; you just have to suck it up and keep it moving.

After going those five months without a visit with them, we had an awesome visit. They've known for a long while that Mommy was in prison for something bad. I never went into details because I felt they were too young. I never intended to keep it a secret because I believe they should know the truth. At this particular visit, my daughter wanted to know exactly why Mommy was in prison. I tried to brush it off and tell her that I did something bad, however, she was very adamant and would not accept that answer. When I realized this was a conversation I couldn't escape, I gave in and this is how the conversation went:

Me: Do you know what selling drugs is?

Her: Yes! It's illegal!

Me: Well, Mommy gave your dad's friends pictures of undercover officers, so that Dad's friends wouldn't sell drugs to the officers and get in trouble.

Her: Why was Dad even hanging out with those type of people? When I get home I am going to say, "What the heck?" Dad should be here, not you.

After that visit, something changed in our relationship. I believe that conversation helped her understand that I want to be home with her. I just can't. My son has always known and we have always had a secure bond. After that, she began to write more and telling me that I am the best mom ever. She was always excited about our phone calls and wanted them to be longer than 15 minutes. That gave me the reassurance that I needed as a mother. One day I was talking to my friend Krystal and expressing my concerns for returning home after being away for so long. I told her if it was going to just be me then it wouldn't be so stressful. However, there are two little people that I am accountable for and I worry about how they will accept me upon my return.

She responded with, "You will take it one day at a time and everything will be fine."

Later that day, I called the kids and they answered the phone so excited to talk to me, which always melts my heart and makes any bad day a great one. Without me asking, they asked if we would relocate away from Jacksonville, which has always been my plan since my arrest. I answered yes. They began to tell me that they would like to be home schooled. I asked them about having friends at school.

At seven years old, my baby girl answered, "The best part about that is we will be home with you and I don't need friends. I am fine by myself." My son quickly agreed. That conversation was just what I needed that day. My Bunkie told me that was a love note from God. He knew my concerns and gave me just what I needed at that moment.

During the time of my incarceration, I've completed the following betterment classes: How to be a Responsible Mother; Empowerment; Domestic & Sexual Violence, Motivation to Change; Recovering from Grief; Recidivism; Anger Management; Cycles of Addiction and a few others. I've completed these courses: Introduction to Veterinary Tech; Poetry; Creative Writing and Toastmasters. I've graduated from the Customer Assistance Technology vocational class. I'm an Aerobics and Fitness Instructor, a Biggest Loser Weight Loss Mentor and I am currently enrolled as a Cosmetology student.

During my time in physical bondage, I've done my best to stay positive and I've never been more free spiritually and mentally. I'll use this stumbling block as a stepping stone. My current situation does not define nor does it determine my future. My biggest and number one supporter is my beautiful mother—truly a gift from God. Without her and God, there is no way I would be able to do this. She keeps me uplifted on a daily basis. Phone calls, books, letters, pictures and anything else I am allowed to have. She makes sure I have everything I need, i.e. soap, toothpaste, deodorant, underwear and shoes. Also everything I want, such as snacks, music for my MP3 player and makeup. The one person I was afraid to call when I got arrested, she is the one I have to call every day. I will forever be grateful for her unconditional mother's love.

To the beautiful young lady reading this… Nothing in life is impossible. You just need the drive to want it. Your current situation does not determine your destiny. Everything happens for a reason. Take it by both hands and turn a negative into a positive. My incarceration has changed my life and I'm allowing it. I encourage you to always reach for your goals and never allow anyone or anything to stand in your way. Have and keep a strong mind and never allow anyone to manipulate you into the opposite direction. Surround yourself with positive individuals with no motives and who always have your best interest at heart. People who are headed in the right direction and want something out of life are the people you want in your life. In any relationship, friendship and even family members, if that individual isn't pushing you forward, they are pulling you backwards and are detrimental to your future. There's no way to move forward if you are held back. If you have no hope with no work, then you have no future. Failure is not an option in my life; don't make it a choice in yours. Always love yourself! If you don't, no one else will.

Men play a major role in women being incarcerated; that's what I've seen during my experience. Whether it's a husband, boyfriend, brother or whatever. Most of the women incarcerated are behind a man, or personal drug abuse. It's crazy. My biological father is deceased and has been since 2008. I was and still am a daddy's girl. I do have an amazing step-father who has been right here fighting to get me home. He is such a blessing to me and my mom. I love him!

To be completely honest with you, I never knew what I did was a crime. Had I known, I would have never done it. I never claimed that I was innocent; I knew that it was unethical. I also know that my sentence was political. I'm still fighting and I pray that God will deliver me from this sooner than later.

After years of appealing her original sentence, in August of 2020, Kenitra was released early from prison and her ten years of probation that she was originally given was terminated. She is now home with her family, happy and hopeful.

Perfectly flawed: Yesterday I did.
Today I can. Tomorrow I will.
Bent and swayed... yet I still remain UNBROKEN!

Chapter 6: Lola

Love is a Hell of a Drug

"Don't sell yourself short playing a supporting role in
someone else's story! Find yourself...
Love yourself...Choose YOURSELF."

As far back as I can remember, drugs have been a part of my life. My earliest memory is pulling at my father's pants leg to get his attention and being swatted away as he gazed at this pill bottle filled with opaque, white chunks, smiling the way I wished he did when he looked at me. I was born in the middle of the crack cocaine era and it took my family by storm. Both my mother and my father lost themselves in an addiction-filled whirlwind that changed the course of all our lives. After seeing what addiction was capable of, I vowed to never do a drug, and even when my friends and peers began to experiment, I kept true to my word and never even smoked a "J". While I personally had no interest in physically taking drugs myself, I found myself drawn to the other side of that world. It's crazy how you can despise something consciously and seek it out subconsciously. Yeah I was a glorified "good girl", but from my very first crush, I found myself attracted to "bad boys". My high school boyfriends were typically low-level weed dealers who dabbed in crack sales here and there. It wasn't the money I was drawn to; it was their attitude and style. When I did date a "good guy", I found him to be boring.

Fast forward to adulthood when I met "Tommy". To my knowledge, he only sold weed—but lots if it—and from the moment he smiled at me, I was his. Tommy had it all: looks, confidence, sense of humor, kindness, and he was well-off. My family hated him and that made me like him even more for some reason. I was in school studying towards my Bachelor's degree and worked a few stints at jobs that I hated. I decided one day to take Tommy up on his offer; he'd been saying I didn't have to work and he was taking care of me anyway. We moved in together and life was great; I became his "counter". I was counting his daily earnings at the end of every night and completing bank runs. I noticed the profits began to increase, but didn't question it or think twice about it. We had it all— nice place, nice cars, ate at the best restaurants and wore the finest designers. What more could a girl ask for? Soon, I had begun to pick up packages for Tommy. When he asked me to, I did it without hesitation. He'd never endanger me or put me in harm's way, I thought. And anyway, it was just weed... right? Three years into our relationship, we'd gone out and the night before, I slept in late. Tommy never did; no matter what, he was up by 7AM. I smelled a strange odor that was so loud I had to get up to see what it was. As I walked in, my mouth dropped. My kitchen was "little Colombia" and there was cocaine everywhere, like a scene from the movie Scarface. Tommy had on gloves and a face mask, breaking the large square packages into smaller ones. I was in shock, but Tommy acted as though it was all normal. He passed me a pair of gloves and instructed me to wrap up the smaller packages, and I did. That was the day everything changed forever. I found out the packages I'd been picking up weren't marijuana after all. I'd been transporting kilos, and for some reason I wasn't outraged or upset; I just accepted it. This drug had found its way back into my life. In a way, it felt like destiny and at least I wasn't using it—that's what I told myself.

Years passed and as we made more and more money, I became more and more involved. I knew the supplier, when it was coming in, how much, and how it was to be distributed. This was definitely not how I imagined I would be using my college degree. One day, on one of my routine pickups, I was almost to my destination and I looked in my rearview mirror. There were at least 10 police cars behind me with flashing lights on. My heart stopped... I was filthy with 17 kilos right in the passenger seat. As I pulled over, the tears rolled and I began to pray. The cops actually sped around me and I couldn't believe it. I just knew I would get caught.

I finished my delivery and told Tommy we needed to talk ASAP. It was at that point I realized how reckless I had become. There were times I'd have a kilo in my purse while running errands, or if we had nowhere to put them quickly, I would store them in my old room at my aunt's house. I was the young, Black, dumb girl riding around with dope in the car and usually 10-30K in her purse. What was I thinking? I wasn't! I told Tommy I was done and he wasn't pleased, but when I asked him how could he allow me to risk so much if he truly loved me, he couldn't answer. I stayed with him, even though he wouldn't stop dealing. We had plenty of cash, but he couldn't stop, and I was reminded of that little girl tugging at her father's pants leg.

Tommy and my father suffered from two different forms of cocaine addiction. Both were chasing an insatiable high that would inevitably lead to their demise. My father chased that high for over two decades, until he became tired enough to quit. He has been sober for six years and counting. However, Tommy chased his way right into the penitentiary. I thank God for waking me up because when people suffer from addictions, they tend to lose sight of what really matters, such as love, respect, right and wrong.

It doesn't matter which side of the high you're on, there will be casualties. Sometimes innocent bystanders get caught in the wrath. So, whether you love a user or a dealer, please choose yourself, because they won't. And it's not that they don't love you or want you; they are just chasing the high. Don't get ran over in the process!

Love,
Lola The Good Girl

Chapter 7: Tiffany, The Grace Messenger

What Is Hope?

In an interview with Diane Sawyer, Tiffany stated, *"It's not over. There is forgiveness and there is hope."*

Romans 5:5 says, *"Now hope does not disappoint, because the love of God has been powered out in our hearts by the Holy Spirit who was given to us, and Colossians 1:27 says "Christ in you, the hope of glory."*

My name is Tiffany and, first and foremost, I'm a Christian. I've been saved since I was in 5th grade. I got saved in vacation bible school, but that was the only time I attended church regularly—that summer of vacation bible school. I didn't grow up in a Christian home. My parents didn't make me go either. They wanted me to choose what I believe. It wasn't until I got locked up in July of 2005 that I really started to look to the Lord to find out who I am and who He is. I ran from the Lord for a long time because man misrepresented God…Jesus, but I always believed in God.

I was one of those who thought God was out to punish me, just waiting to hit me over the head with something the moment I messed up. I thought to myself, if He's like that, why would I run to Him when I need help or anything? I had no example to show me or point me to His true nature. At home, I was taken care of financially—meaning we weren't poor, but we weren't rich either. My family doesn't know anything about encouraging each other and building each other up in love verbally, so negative words flew faster than darts, or nothing at all was said. I can't blame them; they weren't taught verbal acceptance or affirmation either. I couldn't find the love and acceptance I wanted at home, so I sought it on the streets, only to end up finding friends and men who didn't love themselves or others; therefore, they couldn't give me what I sought.

All along I had a void in my heart, that all of you reading this have as well that can only be filled by God. I sought out drugs, alcohol and sex. Drugs and alcohol were what I liked most. I had trust issues with men because the man who was supposed to protect me (my dad), the man I was supposed to trust the most, had violated that trust when I was in high school my freshman year. Right after that my best friend slept with my first boyfriend that I bought home and had a real relationship with, there was another violation of trust from a guy close to me. My start clearly wasn't the best.

Right before I got locked up, my dad had been battling cancer and at the last doctor's appointment he went to when I was around, they told him he had one more line of chemo and if that didn't work there was nothing they could do for him. That news shook me. On top of that, my dad was a big man, probably 236 pounds with big arms, but he was scared and I could tell. My dad had started going to church and even tried to get me to go. My dad wanted to live, but he wasn't sure he would, otherwise he wouldn't have been so scared. I saw fear in him and it hurt me to the core. I couldn't stand to see him suffer.

I started hanging out with my co-defendant whom I'd just met and stayed gone with him for three weeks, then I was incarcerated on these murder charges. My dad passed away three months after I got locked up. The Lord had been speaking to me in April of 2005. A pastor and his wife were speaking to me at 2AM as I was high as a kite on the couch bawling my eyes out because me and my boyfriend had been fighting so much. I was miserable. I knew there was more to life and I wanted the change that these two pastors on TV were speaking of. So, when I got locked up three months later, I picked up a bible on the first night of incarceration in the dorm and started looking to the Lord. I had to keep looking to Him and standing on His word to get through the trial and sentencing. It was hard to sit there and listen to death sentences being handed down but, somehow, I still had peace that this would turn around. At the sentencing phase, which took place six months after the trial, I was the one walking away telling my family, "It ain't over", as they started crying. I already had time to prepare. It was either going to be life or death, so I knew what to expect.

Before I got locked up when my dad was battling cancer, the hope I heard about was the same kind of hope I heard about being preached in the Duval County Jail. That "hope" was "hope" for the best, but expect the worst. To be honest, that didn't bring me hope at all. I just stood on the peace I had and the word from Jeremiah 29:11 I had received right after opening my bible that first night in captivity.

In 2011, after being here on death row for three years, a TBN satellite was hooked up so I could access Christian television all the time. Long story short, I finally found someone preaching the gospel of grace—the good news based solely on Jesus and his finished work on the cross. A hope that has nothing to do with me but everything to do with Him, Jesus the hope of glory on the inside of me. Since Jesus is the hope of glory, the word clearly details what hope is. Hope doesn't disappoint. Also if you study the new testament, the word hope in Greek is the word "elpis", which means confident expectation of good. This tells me that what most people believe hope to be is an uncertainty and a shakable foundation. Because of Christ in me, and any of you who will simply believe in Christ, we can stand firm on His love and favor and know that no matter what the world says or what the courts say, THINGS WILL WORK OUT FOR GOOD. I hope for big things because you're sure to get it through the holy spirit in you! Even if you don't see it now, you will have a blessed life, family, career, marriage, ministry and health *because the power lives in you! Jesus loves you and He will manifest what He suffered and died for you to have!*

2 Corinthians 3:17 says, "where the spirit of the Lord is there is freedom", so all of you who are incarcerated— whether physically or spiritually—freedom already lives inside of you. The inside has to manifest to the outside. Keep hoping in hope! You are forgiven of all sin past, present and future, that's why the hope of glory can live in you. Trust Him and He will break every chain! Jesus has done it all for you on the cross!

The gospel of grace, Jesus, the hope of glory has changed me from the inside out and proven how real He is to me in so many ways. I know how much He loves me. I know how valuable and worthy I am of real love and I know for certain He's delivered me from drugs and alcohol. I know for certain I'm worthy of making the right man wait for marriage before sex and I know for certain He will deliver me from captivity. To say otherwise is to dishonor God's son Jesus' work on the cross. I'd rather believe this truth rather than believing a loving God who died for me may or may not ransom me when the word redemption is all about paying the price to buy me out of the power of another by the power of his blood shed on the cross. (Gal 3:13) Anyone willing to trust God more than man and hope that the hope of glory will make everything good and see freedom manifest?

If I could say anything to my younger self, I'd tell her that when God brought you into this world He gave you a fingerprint that isn't like anyone's walking this planet for a reason. He made you different and special, so stop trying to be like everyone else; you were made to stand out, not fit in. Younger Tiffany, you were never going to fit in! You're going to grow up and be a boss, a leader, and leaders lead not follow. I'd tell girls following down the same path that I did that the truth is you are a beautiful butterfly that has only landed in rubbish. You don't have to let the hurts and muck of life stain or stick to your wings. Flap that stuff off and fly! What I've learned is that I have to FIRST know how God sees me and know He loves me. He always sees me as that beautiful butterfly soaring through the air and that when people don't like you or try to pull you down, you can shake it off like water off a duck's back and keep flying high.

I've learned that everyone's NOT gonna like me and that's OK. Those people probably don't like themselves and they're the insecure ones trying to project all their negativity my way. I'd tell girls all over the world that when God created you, He created you with value and worth before you could do anything to deserve it or not deserve it. Life was meant to be enjoyed and when you don't know your value and worth and know how much God loves you, the world can pull you down into their rubbish. What "THE CLIQUE" says is not who you are. It's what you believe about yourself that matters most, so why not go to the one who created you to find out instead of man who will praise you one day and crucify you the next day? God's opinion of you will never change. That truth is found in Jesus if you will only believe!

REALIZE: SELF-ESTEEM is about how you see yourself. It has nothing to do with how others see you! Find ways to build you up and not let others tell you who you are or define you.

Chapter 8: Jhody

From Nothing To Everything

"Outside I was just the fat girl on drugs trying to lose weight so I can be pretty. I can only imagine if I would have stayed on the streets who I would have become. A lot of people be like, "Oh you don't wanna glorify prison and make it seem like prison is good"… I'm not saying that at all, but shit my conditions was just as bad where I came from, so in a way that didn't really impact me as bad as it has some other people. I always learned to take nothing and make it out of something. I did the same thing with prison; I took that shit and I turned it into an experience that was amazing. The older I get, the more I realize that it isn't really what happened in prison; it's what prison prepared me for. You have to use it. It's a day-by-day choice to be a good person—a person that contributes to the community."

As result of my advocacy, I am always added to prison interest groups on social media, in particular, Lowell Correctional Institution Family and Friends. Within this group, the families of those being housed at Lowell share their experiences, provide support and their grievances. Jhody made a post one day sharing her story and I sent her a friend request. She mentioned that while in prison she had been a law clerk. At the time I befriended her, I wasn't actively working on the book. I have learned that Jhody is a voice for all the women left behind, as well as a change agent. Just recently, she was chosen as an Open Society Foundations Soros Justice Fellow and 1.4 million dollars was awarded to 16 fellows to fund their respective initiatives. Jhody will support incarcerated law clerk programs around the country and develop a network that will mentor those seeking legal careers upon their release from prison.

Jhody wants people to know that law clerks don't just work on legal issues within the criminal justice system. They provide assistance with immigration and family law, helping women get their rights back to their children once they are released from prison. During the spring of 2018, I attended a peace building training and, coincidentally, Jhody was there. She introduced herself by her Department of Corrections number. I immediately became emotional because, although free, she hadn't lost touch with the identifier she was known by for seven long years. Seven years of not being called by her government name. Seven years away from her children. Seven years spent rebuilding herself and retrieving everything that was stolen from her since childhood.

"At a young age, I learned that being smart was a curse. I used to get a lot of awards and write poetry in elementary school. I used to get teased so much for being smart. I was overweight. I didn't have name brand clothes and the few friends I had were white. Being fat and smart made me ugly and a target to my Black peers. Eventually, my need to fit in with them became more important than academics."

Jhody wasn't skinny and popular, therefore, didn't fit into the normal Black girl persona; she adopted a tough male persona instead. This didn't mean she liked girls, but developed a homeboy attitude. Her male peers were not interested in her physically. To prove herself, she acted tough. She stopped being the girl getting pushed over and became the big girl that would push back. This role was solidified for her at age ten through forming a club; the initiation was to steal from the nearby dollar and grocery store. Other kids would steal items such as nails, toys and food and give them to her.

As the bully who was always suspended, Jhody began getting into more fights at school. There is not a yearbook picture of her after 6th grade because most of the fights occurred around that time. At home, Jhody had both parents until the age of eleven and two younger brothers. Her youngest brother was in and out of the house. When he was eleven, he went to a disciplinary program for youth, then again at seventeen. Today he is serving a 30-year prison sentence.

Once Jhody's mom and dad separated, her brothers would often go stay at her dad's house and Jhody would be home alone. When they finally divorced, this gave her an opportunity to live the way she wanted to. Jhody would allow girls to come over and spend the night and bring company over, which included sneaking boys in. The name brand clothes and shoes she wanted, she would just steal them. And being sexually active brought the attention from boys that ignored her in elementary school.

At age fifteen, Jhody had a boyfriend and her mom allowed him to move in with them. He was four years older than her and had a car and a job. Jhody soon realized she wasn't meant to be in a relationship and didn't find interest in being a good girl. Coldhearted, the streets had taught her to not care about or need anyone else but herself.

Jhody was articulate and smart, which helped her get jobs and work consistently since the age of fourteen. She maintained above average grades in high school but, due to lack of attendance, was unable to earn all of her credits. In 2002, she walked across the stage with her graduating class, yet never received a diploma. Jhody enrolled as a Dual Enrollment student at Santa Fe College (SFC) during her Junior year and eventually received her GED in 2004 after the birth of her son. Falling in love with the streets at ten impelled her to put that love and loyalty over everything. Her world consisted of becoming and furthering the Thug Life culture she grew up and lived in. After getting her GED she became a bail bondsman, while still pursuing a dental assisting degree at SFC. Being in and from the streets made her a popular bail bondsman; she also didn't require collateral. She was making more money than she could have imagined and this only encouraged extravagant spending and excessive drug use. Finally acquiring money, power, and recognition, Jhody was taking care of herself, her family, and the whole neighborhood.

In 2006, ecstasy pill use exploded in the local Gainesville Black neighborhoods. Jhody began taking ecstasy pills after giving birth to her daughter in 2006 to lose weight, but soon became addicted. As the bail bondsman, drugs and money came fast and easy. Before her incarceration in 2007, she was taking 15 to 25 pills a day.

Jhody never imagined being in a relationship with her daughter's father when they met. He looked just like the rapper T.I. and she never believed he would fall in love, let alone be interested in a long-term relationship with her. It was a total surprise when he asked her to have his baby. They became Bonnie and Clyde, but as expected, their relationship was toxic and filled with drama.

When Jhody became pregnant, not only did she find out that he had another lady; he disappeared until after the baby was born. He called her once during the pregnancy, claiming to want to be with her, but after she sent him the money to return home, he stopped answering and disconnected his phone. When he showed up three months after the birth, he immediately began reaping the benefits of her lifestyle. She generously supplied for both her pill addiction and his cocaine addiction. Although an addict, Jhody was making money, owned two trucks, and was taking care of herself, family, and her two small kids. She was the smallest she had ever been and the world was hers for the taking.

Bonnie and her Clyde started getting pulled over a lot by the police, and each time there were drugs in the car, he would take the charges. A few times the kids were in the car and had they both gone to jail, her children would have been taken from her. Jhody's bail bondsman job title allowed her to immediately bond him out. After his second arrest for her drugs in the truck, he told Jhody that he was not going to attend the court dates. She decided to leave Gainesville and run with him; they packed up the kids and headed to his birth city of Tampa. On the outside Jhody was a young professional and college student who also worked the night shift at a local convenience store. Once her daughter's father returned to her life, it was a fast, descent down. She was literally killing herself trying to maintain.

Not soon after moving to Tampa, Jhody and her daughter's father were pulled over and the police discovered that he had a warrant in Alachua County where they had just left. He was arrested and transported back to Gainesville. Jhody was determined to get him out of jail and to get out of the state of Florida. She came up with a plan to break into the safe at her job. The money would assist with getting him out and escaping far away. Her former boss already suspected something, so he placed cameras in the office. Jhody noticed the cameras and after stealing the money out of the safe, set the place on fire. There was only $75 in the safe, which prompted another plan: stealing a car and selling it to the chop shop.

Jhody had a great aunt who was elderly so she went to her house to try and steal her car. An attempt at hotwiring it was unsuccessful, so she broke in, tied her up and took the keys. Jhody had just turned twenty-three years old in January of 2007. The crimes were committed on April 20th and on April 21st she turned herself in.

Charged with arson, larceny, grand theft auto and home invasion robbery, Jhody was never able to get her daughter's father out. He was soon released after sharing letters with the State that linked Jhody and her motives to the crimes. The State made it very clear that if the case went to trial, she would lose and be sentenced to life in prison. Accepting her guilty actions, Jhody couldn't gamble with her life and took a State plea for 13 years; eight years in prison followed by five years' probation. Jhody stayed in the county jail from April to September of 2007. She was transferred to Lowell Annex in Ocala, Florida, in November of 2007.

The first thing she noticed when off the bus was the sky. It was like seeing it for the first time. Jhody had been tall all her life and was given prison uniforms that were not in the best conditions; she also wore a size 13 shoe. Remembering the underwear provided being nasty, the mattresses stained with blood, urine and feces, she humbly reflects, "*It was in prison that I learned healthy hygiene practices. By watching other women, I started taking pride in myself.*"

In 2008, Jhody was shipped over four hours from home to her permanent camp at Gadsden C.I. It was there that she was assigned to train and work as a certified inmate law clerk. She would serve a little over two years at G.C.I before going back to Lowell on a good adjustment transfer. Once back at Lowell, Jhody became the confinement law clerk. There, she got to peek into the souls of women in solitary confinement and death row. At this time there was only one woman on death row: Tiffany, The Grace Messenger. Jhody describes Tiffany as thoughtful, funny and amazing. Tiffany would minister and mentor Jhody through her cell door.

"*It was one of the most beneficial relationships to me in prison. I'm thankful every day that I got the opportunity to be in there with those women to the point that I don't forget that there are hundreds of thousands of strong women that are incarcerated. In prison, I unlearned all of the lies that I had believed about myself and I was able to fall in love with myself and decide who I wanted to be.*"

During Jhody's incarceration, her mother and children were homeless often. In the beginning of her sentence, Jhody, her mother and both her siblings were all incarcerated at the same time. Her two children were sent to stay with an aunt. Out of the seven years that Jhody served, she saw her children maybe six times.

"Out of sight, out of mind works both ways", Jhody says. At the time of her arrest, her daughter was only three months old and her son two years old. She remembers, after three years in, secretly waiting for her family to leave when they surprised her with a visit. They had become strangers and the inside walls had become her home and community. During her first year of prison, her grandmother financially supported her, but once she died there wasn't much other than what her father could send her on occasion... *"God just always made a way for me through those years."*

Within a month of her release in 2014, Jhody became employed as a housekeeper at a Motel 6 where she worked for two and a half years, earning a promotion from housekeeper to front desk manager during that time. With the authority to hire employees, preference was given to other women with criminal backgrounds and Jhody used it as an opportunity to not just give women a job, but to build the same support system that existed among women in prison.

Instead of judging them, she helped them and made the Motel 6 a safe place to learn, grow, and get through their tough shifts and lives. Jhody came home wanting to be a lawyer, enrolling in the College of Central Florida and pursuing her A.S. degree in paralegal studies to prepare for law school.

In 2016, Jhody met Desmond Meade, founder of the Florida Rights Restoration Coalition. She accepted an invite to a retreat in Orlando, Florida, although terrified because she had never left her hometown before and the thought triggered her anxiety. This was her first experience being around empowered, formerly incarcerated people and leaders. The experience changed her within. In 2017, Jhody joined the National Council for Incarcerated and Formerly Incarcerated Women and Girls and took her first flight to the inaugural FreeHer Conference in New York. Little did she realize that this would be the first flight of many traveling all over the country and world advocating for communities and women like her, both in and out of prisons.

Although free, there were still barriers to overcome. While working at Motel 6 Jhody was doing well but had reached her limit, so she took a fearful leap, leaving that job to find another as a convicted felon in Florida. She landed a job in another county at a Quality Inn making $8.50 an hour. The 45-minute commute from home was taking a toll on her, so she moved closer to her new job. This, too, was a process because it was hard to find a landlord that wanted to rent to her with a blemished past. Jhody had chosen to not return back to Alachua County immediately after her release and stayed in Ocala after prison where she met Mr. Rock Saunders, a landlord and retired cop, who took a chance on her. Jhody is still very appreciative of the opportunity that he gave her when many would not.

Parenting after incarceration was not initially easy either. Her children were now seven and nine years old. Jhody was also married within a year of her release; however, the marriage only lasted three years. Reintegrating with her family and children she says was the toughest barrier to date to overcome.

"Take the time to get to know yourself and take the time to figure out what you want and what you like, what you need and what you don't like so that you are comfortable with yourself. Don't be afraid to change your mind. If one week something you like is different, that's OK. I wish I had given myself the same chance I gave every guy, every man, every homegirl. I wish I had given myself just as much attention and a fighting chance. Fight for yourself. Don't give up and don't count the failures as impossible evidence of who you are or what you can achieve. When we fail, it makes us so much stronger. I encourage other women because it also encourages me. Be selfish with yourself. Find the space within yourself and

outside of yourself where it isn't about anybody but you. We are most of the time caught up being someone's mother, girlfriend, partner, caretaker, their everything and we forget to be ourselves and good to ourselves. None of that [matters] if you aren't good with you. Women are some of the greatest gifts the world has ever received."

Chapter 9: Amanda

Addicted To The Hustle

"I'm 30 years old and look where I'm at."

Amanda was raised in a two-parent household. As a small child, her father served time in prison for possession with the intent to manufacture. After he was released from prison, he started driving trucks and would be away from home five to six days a week. This left her mom to raise her and her siblings alone for the most part, although Dad was there financially. At age nine Amanda's half brother, whom she shared a father with, began molesting her and this went on for two years before anyone found out. Amanda was afraid to tell then, but bravely confesses in one of her letters:

"*After being molested, I felt alone, like no one was helping. What was I to do but cry on them lonely nights? Nobody knew the pain that changed my life. Thinking who was I to tell and what would they think of me...*" Amanda's mom noticed her behavior change and threatened to take her to the doctor where he could tell if anyone had touched her. Terrified of what the visit may entail, Amanda told her parents what had been happening. They confronted her brother and he denied it. Afterwards, he went to live with his mother and that was the end of it.

By age fourteen Amanda was very promiscuous and seeking the attention of men. Her only means of help were her parents and by this time her mother had developed a crack addiction. She met her first child's father on the corner of her block selling weed; they became cool and started getting high together. Shortly after they became boyfriend and girlfriend, she found herself pregnant. He would get locked up almost every single week. On the day of her baby shower, he went to jail and wasn't released until her son was three years old. Amanda was also playing the role of mother to her sixteen-year-old brother, twelve-year-old sister and sixteen-year-old cousin while her mom served time for selling drugs.

Just when she thought things couldn't get any worse, a very bad car accident almost ended her life. Accustomed to making sure the house was clean, helping with schoolwork, shopping and doing laundry, beyond home, Amanda was out of control.

She met a guy who would end up being her second child's father; he was madly in love with Amanda since the day they bumped into each other walking to school. He worked a job and hustled every now and then. During this time, she was partying, drinking and smoking weed. Her dad was more of a friend than a father, so behavioral expectations weren't enforced. With Mom in jail and Dad working a lot, Amanda turned to a drug dealer for love and support. Once he was arrested, Amanda took over his drug corners for a few years and was able to feed her kids by selling drugs. Over the course of a three-year span, Amanda was arrested fifteen times. When she was released after the last offense, her third child's father was arrested for murder.

There was a meter maid who lived on Amanda's street and monitored the drug activity on the block. She would allow the police to watch the dealers from her window. One day she rode past Amanda's house while she and her friends were on the porch and one of them yelled "Bitch". The cops were called and Amanda was arrested for several charges, but only one of them stuck. She plead guilty to terroristic threats and was given six to twenty-three months in jail, but was released after nine months.

The second time Amanda was arrested was for fighting a girl; they both talked to the same guy and fought on the porch of the girl's home. The other girl already had wounds from another incident, but during the fight one of the wounds re-opened and it appeared to the cops it was a result of Amanda hitting her. The girl also told the police that she was robbed. Amanda was three months pregnant on probation and taken back to jail. After several months of court hearings, the victim never appeared so the case was dropped. While awaiting the outcome of this case Amanda gave birth to her third baby in jail. She explained to me via an email from Corrlinks, a Federal prison emailing platform:

"I was having contractions at like 8 a.m. I went about the day until it got worse. When I realized I was in labor, I was sent out and within forty-five minutes I went from three centimeters to ten. Five minutes after getting to the hospital, my leg was cuffed to the bed. I had natural labor with a C.O. next to me. I stayed for twenty-four hours and was sent back. I had to leave my baby and couldn't call nobody to make sure they would pick her up. When I got back from the hospital, it was twelve hours before I got a call to make sure my baby was picked up. My mother picked the baby up after I snuck and gave someone my phone time and Mom's info to make sure they knew what was going on and to be alert for the call to pick the baby up."

Free again, but still addicted to the hustle, Amanda started running with drug dealers all over the country. Her home was even shot up. Although living the fast life, she was jail and trouble-free for about eight years until she met a low-key baller who was trafficking cocaine, unbeknownst to her. He introduced her to running money to the West Coast with all expenses paid. She was compensated for picking up disclosed drugs and was living the good life, or so she thought. One day while in Baltimore they were stopped by Homeland Security. Her co-defendant had convinced her to sign for a package using her real name. There were four of them, but only three were arrested. Amanda was the only girl arrested and charged with conspiracy to deliver cocaine. He paid $8,000 towards her bail and that was it; he never offered her any other help and left her high and dry. They all ended up taking a universal plea. Amanda received thirty months, the Kingpin received five years and the other co-defendant served three years. The fourth girl was never charged.

"To look back on my reality. I did it all for the love, just to have all the finer things and be on top of my game. My mom was my shelter but I broke free. My body was big but far from grown. I was broke down from the things men used to say to me... Never be afraid to reach out for help. No matter what the situation is, it can save your life. Don't be afraid to fight your fears. In the long run it will torture your mind, at least it did [for me]. Never settle for less and know your worth. Put no one above you. You see, you are perfect regardless of what anyone else says. Nobody should make you feel pressured to do anything they themselves would not do. Selling dreams to naïve kids, who am I to blame except myself? Respect yourself in life and don't be consumed with hate. Choose to see through the negative things that life throws your way. I'm thirty years old and look where I'm at. Starting life over and I thank the Lord every day and pray there's no turning back. I want to remain happy with my family and that's a fact. The things I have done in the past it's too late to regret. I have just learned from my mistakes in the past. I took from the good and the bad and it helped build me into who I am now. I have been through a lot of different phases to find my way and now I know my happy days are not far away. I sit back and look at what it took for me to get here, what I have to show for it and who is still by my side when the smoke clears. I was forced into a situation to be a woman. I never really cared about nothing but money, drugs and partying. As I got older, it became worse. My actions became bolder and my heart got colder and I had a chip on my shoulder and I dared anybody to touch it. I knew if I became strong enough I would live long enough to see my kids do something more constructive with their lives and not

go down the path I did. I was another statistic headed nowhere fast is how I see it now. I was possessed by the darker side, living a dangerous life. It wasn't long before I hit rock bottom looking at how the streets had me wide open. I'm glad to say prison saved my life. I couldn't find the willpower to change my life myself. I got nothing but love for those who know how it feels and much respect for those who kept it real. The ones who stayed strong through my stubbornness and persuaded me from doing wrong, and for my parents and family that stuck with me through it all. They get all of my respect because it's due. Most importantly, to my four children: thank you for loving me through this. I changed for you."

Chapter 10: Anonymous

Walking by Faith

"Walking by faith requires a strong determination to follow God's plan, regardless of what life throws your way. You know it's a higher power when the mountain is moved. I had to totally surrender and let God take the wheel."

M*y life changed in the blink of an eye on July 15, 2000. An argument escalated into a physical altercation, resulting in me wearing a pair of silver handcuffs. W-H-Y? I cried out so many times asking God 'WHY' and the answer received was, Why not you? [I was] alone, barefoot, sitting in the back of a police cruiser wondering what just happened. Traumatized… in a state of disbelief are words that come to mind when I reflect on the events of the early morning hours. My one phone call was to my parents who lived 3 hours away, letting them know I was being charged with the murder of my husband.*

The journey began with fingerprints, photographs, issued uniformed etc. and I was escorted to what would be my temporary living space. Totally outside of my environment, the jailhouse chatter is, "Don't let the public defender's office represent you." My choices were limited, especially since my parents and I were unfamiliar with the judicial process. I had to swallow any pride and accept help from those reaching out. My small circle of friends and co-workers, at the time, stepped up and showed support—from collecting funds and just being available to help where needed.

The judicial system is slow and the PD office is overloaded with cases. My case came along a little over a year after the 10-20-Life Florida Statutes law went into effect, coupled with being an election year. My legal team led by Mr.

Patrick McGuinness with the Public Defender's office had their hands full.

It would be remiss of me to not share with you what I fully understand now to know I was a victim of Domestic Violence.

The **legal definition** *for domestic violence is found at Fla. Statute 741.28:*

1) *"Domestic Violence" means any assault,* aggravated assault, battery, aggravated battery, sexual assault, sexual battery, stalking, aggravated stalking, kidnapping, false imprisonment, or any criminal offense resulting in physical injury or death of one family or household member or another household member.

2) "Family or Household Member" means spouses, former spouses, persons related by blood or marriage, persons who are presently residing together as if a family or who have resided together in the past as if a family, and persons who are parents of a child in common regardless of whether they have been married. With the exception of persons who have a child in common, the family or household members must be currently residing or have in the past resided together in the same single dwelling unit.

Domestic Violence is not a topic of conversation openly discussed and it doesn't only affect a certain group of people. Many people don't believe they even know someone who is experiencing any form of abuse to include, but not limited to: physical, sexual, emotional, financial or social isolation. **Domestic Violence is about Power and Control.**
Did I believe my husband was abusing me to the point of filing a police report? Did I tell anyone he would be out of control when he drank? Did I? Short answer: "NO". The question always asked is: why not tell? My reason for not disclosing doesn't change the fact that he wasn't given the right to be emotionally/physically abusive (i.e. infidelity, hit, slapped, beaten, disciplined, etc.).
My legal team was effective in getting me in the home detention program, while I awaited trial. Understand as you're going through the judicial process you're closely watched and everything is subject to scrutiny. I recall the Prosecutor contacting my best friend, now husband, and questioning our conversations. At the time, it seemed like every obstacle presented itself in an effort to break my spirit. The jury ruled against me and the judge sentenced me to football years. To this day, I don't speak of the number of years because it wasn't something I allowed my spirit to accept. To say I was crushed is a misstatement.
When I was taken back to the jail, I was placed on suicide watch. Imagine being in a cell with a wrap to clothe your body, stripped of everything. I cried so hard, my eyes were swollen; I wasn't eating and not allowed any visitors. I had to prove I wasn't a harm to myself or others before being released from solitary confinement. During this time, I had to dig deep down and find the will to continue, despite what I was seeing... **Walk by Faith, not by Sight.**

I had to wrap my head around being transported to the Women's Correctional Facility. My spirit was defeated at this time. While others on the transport bus seemed excited, asking "How much time do you have?" my response was, "It doesn't matter because I'm not doing this time." That shut all conversation down. My goal was to be in the environment but not become the environment. I hung onto the hopes that my district court appeal would be granted and this nightmare would end. I had to start preparing myself mentally for a battle. The time for crying and asking 'WHY' was over.

The weak will fall prey. Therefore, I spent my free time in the law library, reading and getting a better understanding of the process. During the time my case was on appeal, it seemed like time slowed to a crawl. Keeping myself occupied was a necessity.

In 2006, my Appellate Attorney argued errors in the second trial, but the district court did not rule in my favor. Reading the words from a paid attorney that there was "Nothing else he could do" and "Good Luck" (not exactly like that, but how I perceived the message), [was devastating]. I had another inmate offer assistance in the process, but the stakes were high. My trust barometer was at an all-time low and it was getting harder on my support system. Letters got fewer, funds lesser and greater time between visits. However, in November of 2007, two weeks after my father's passing, Mr. Pat McGuiness called me to share the Supreme Court of Florida overturned my previous convictions. With mixed emotions, I was elated yet sad that my father wasn't alive to see this moment.

There were many things to consider at this pivotal point. What got me to this point? **Walking by Faith, not by Sight***. I entered into an agreement with the State for time served in prison with eight years, no early termination probation. Each time my case was reversed, the State wasn't happy. Although there were no indicators of re-offending, the* *no early termination clause was a tough pill to swallow. Under normal circumstances, after successfully completing half of your sentence you can petition the court for early termination. If at any point I violated, my probation would be revoked and I'd return to complete the balance of the time originally sentenced. Needless to say, violation was not a part of my plan.*

In December 2011, Mr. Pat McGuinness and another friend eagerly awaited my release. As we drove away, playing loudly in the car was Ray Charles' song "Hit the Road Jack". Twenty-three days before my probation was due to expire, I received a signed order from the judge that my probation officer had violated me. I read that piece of paper numerous times as if the words would be different. I had just checked in with her a couple of days prior and she said NOTHING. How can this be happening? My mind is reflecting back over the past years, reading the original probation order, what did I miss? I paid a total of $12,099.10 (for eight months, I paid $225.00) before I became gainfully employed, successfully completed 200 community service hours and integrated back into society. I had to get real and dig deep within. I had no clue what the justification was for violating me this close to the end.

When the probation officer accepted my call, she stated that I could explain to the judge why $5,000.00 in restitution wasn't paid. I had no control over how the money was disbursed between cost of supervision, court fees and fines. As stated in the order, I had to appear before the judge and by my side was Mr. Pat McGuinness. In the courtroom was my friend, retired Probation Officer, and in spirit many positive thoughts and prayers. Again, the wheels of justice move slowly; it was following the money and proving to the judge that the money was paid though not applied correctly. I had to appear one last time before the judge for the decision. Standing alongside me, Pat, and in the courtroom my friend, we heard the judge rule in my favor and terminate my *probation. An exhale moment. I gave a silent thank-you to the court officer who confirmed the money was paid.*

Twenty years have passed since that blink of an eye. I can't say my eyes don't tear up when I recall certain painful events, because I will always have those internal scars. Domestic Abuse crosses all barriers, socio-economic levels, races and cultures. Society is hearing about more and more cases of domestic violence from celebrities, athletes and your neighbor down the street. Break the silence and reach out to your local Domestic Violence Center or call the National Domestic Violence Hotline at 1-800-799-7233.

*When Renata reached out to me seven years ago to be a part of her journey, I wasn't at a point in my life to share. I know our purpose for crossing paths was not by chance. What happened to me can happen to anyone. If my words touch one life, I have fulfilled the **why me***.

Walk by Faith and not by Sight

Chapter 11: Shawneequa

Shattered Woman

*"Our scars are reminders that the path is real
and we no longer live there anymore."*

More than three years ago, I received correspondence from a young man serving a life sentence named Halim Flowers. Although behind bars, Halim has many accolades, as well as a social presence. He has authored more than ten books. He is a poet, was featured on an Emmy-Award-winning HBO documentary, sits on the board of a non-profit and uses his life as an example for the youth, as well as a voice for the many young men like him in prisons all over the world. Initially, when I began corresponding with Halim he told me that he had a friend assisting him with all of his efforts.

After a while, I found out that Halim would email Shawneequa and she would in turn send me the messages. Eventually, we spoke when she was passing me a message and we began to speak regularly. I shared with her that I was working on a project about female incarceration, which inspired her to open up about her troubled past, spending five years in a juvenile facility. In my opinion, Shawneequa is the poster child for how a relationship with men totally affects your life—from age six, manipulated by a trusted man in the neighborhood, to her mother's boyfriends sexually molesting her and nothing being done about it, to ending up in a physically abusive marriage. Today, she has zero trust in men and prefers platonic, non-physical relationships with them.

In her words: *Being born into a broken and un-nurtured foundation breeds the same chaotic beginning. I was given life by two teenaged parents: a mother who has no sense of identity of self and father who thought charm and good* looks would get him through life. My earliest memory of childhood had to be around age three; my mother was big and pregnant. It was right after Christmas. She left for a week or so and upon her return came back light—empty belly and empty arms. For years, I wondered why she came back in that condition. What happened? Later, I would discover the truth. In February of 1984, my mother gave birth to my brother and gave him up for adoption. My mother was a mere 15-year-old young lady that became a mother, yet never embodied the responsibilities of the position. My house was never a safe place for me because my mother always had men around partying, or would pull her disappearing acts. She began to disappear around nineteen years old; I was four. We were living with my grandparents. My grandfather had a tradition of not eating until everyone was home. Eventually, my grandfather stopped waiting on her to show up and we would have dinner without her.

At age five, my mom and I moved into our own apartment. I remember there being kids to play with, a pool and a playground. I didn't have to deal with my mom because I could go outside and play. As long as my mom had male company, she would be OK, but the minute problems arose with them, she began to mistreat me. Women would come to the house and confront her about her inappropriate dealings with their man. I can recall her blaming me when things would occur.

In Kindergarten, Shawneequa's mom had a male companion whose name was Bill. Bill was nice and brought food over and invited Shawneequa to sit with them and eat. This infuriated her mother because this took away from her time alone with Bill. Shawneequa's mom told her to hurry up and finish and go back to the room. When she finished and was en route back to her room, her mom slapped her in the back of the head. Back in the room, Shawneequa hid in the closet. While hiding, she could hear Bill and her mom arguing.

The TV was blasting in her mom's room, so she went in to turn the volume down and no one was there. The next morning, Shawneequa woke up, got dressed for school, walked to the bus stop and came back home and ate cold weenies and bologna. After about six days, her mom returned as if nothing had happened, told her that she missed her and bought her a Cabbage Patch Kids doll. It was also around this time that Shawneequa met her biological father. After meeting him initially, she didn't see him again until she was ten years old. He took her to a drug house all day and promised to take her somewhere fun. Later in the evening, he attempted to take her on a shopping spree, but the store was closed.

I was six years old when the mailman asked me to help him with putting mail in the boxes. It made me feel needed. As I helped him put the mail in the boxes for the neighborhood, he exposed himself to me and told me that it was my reward for helping him. When I told my mom, she said, "Leave me alone, I have company."

I had a new 'uncle' every week and there were a few that were very nice to me and my mother. There were parties every weekend and I became an unofficial bartender fixing drinks. I would fix drinks while my mother drove down the highway and once home she would wake me out of my sleep to fix drinks at the parties. By the time I was in second grade, everything got worse. My mom had a boyfriend named Raymond who was very abusive. Every time Mom and Raymond fought, she would literally get in the car and go look for him. During one incident, Raymond was in the restroom beating my mom so badly that she peed in the bed because she had been holding it so long. My mom exited the restroom battered and bruised badly. I walked on eggshells at home and did what I needed to do in school out of fear of Raymond and my mom. It's like she needed her own personal punching bag because she was having to be one for everyone else.

Shawneequa loved elementary school. She was in the choir, delivered the morning announcements and in fifth grade was selected to be in a Broadway play "Ain't Misbehaving", in which only ten kids were chosen. However, her grandmother was the only one who attended. Her mom never showed up to any events. At age nine, Shawneequa was molested by her older cousin. She never talked about it until this project and shared with me that years later she confronted him about it; he said that he committed the act because he loved her.

In middle school, Shawneequa became the best actress in the world. Her mother's drinking was out of control, the drug addiction increased, along with her attachments to men. Her mom had a boyfriend named Derrick and he tried to make her call him "Daddy". He was always in and out of jail and her mom faithfully visited him each time, even though he was abusive to her when he was home. One day while in the seventh grade, Shawneequa's mother picked her up from school for a family emergency; Derrick had been arrested again in Denton, Texas, and was in jail for about a year. While visiting Derrick, a woman tapped Shawneequa on the shoulder and told her a man was trying to get her attention. Her mom was so engrossed in conversation she didn't even notice she had gotten up to walk over and speak with this guy. It was her biological father and when her mom finally turned around, he blew a kiss at her. Then, he and Derrick began arguing.

I was 13 years old when I was given the harsh reality that my mother didn't want anything to do with me unless it benefited her. Derrick was out and we went to Dallas to visit his mom. She lived close to a girl that I met previously when I had gone to her house to help with the church bulletins. Her name was Shaniqua, too. I learned the truth about my mother to this day that makes me despise her. My mother's boyfriend, Derrick, raped me as she laid next to him asleep. I yelled for him to get off of me and she told me to shut up and that I had to learn about it anyway. Not only was my body broken, so was what was left of my heart. I lost all hope in life and those that surrounded me saying that they loved and cared for me.

Almost six months later, I was arrested and sent to a juvenile prison. I was sentenced to nine months and instead I spent almost five years there. I purposely missed my release date because I had nothing to come home to. I was incarcerated from age 13 to 18 and can count on one hand how many times my mother visited. There were two counselors at Texas Youth Commission who gave me a sense of escape. They both encouraged me and told me what I had encountered didn't define who I was. If it weren't for them I would not have cared about what happened to me. While serving my time, I tried to kill myself because I was better off being in the ground and out of everyone's life altogether. No one wanted me anyway; I was only good for someone to use as their punching bag, sex toy, source of benefits, someone to take care of them etc… but what about me? Who will care for me? Who will love me? Why do you hurt me? Why wasn't I ever good enough? I would do anything just so you would love me or at least acknowledge me. Why?

In 2019, Shawneequa resided in Marietta, California, in horrible living conditions and didn't have custody of her children. She had been awarded a housing voucher but the waiting list was years long. Having a home was the answer to all of her problems to regain custody of her children so she researched other states that would take her voucher and Tennessee was one of them. It helped because she had a friend there who she had been corresponding with during his incarceration. In February of 2019 she decided to relocate and moved with "Junior's" sister until he was released from prison. The relocation was a fresh start for her in a new place and seemingly life was moving in a new direction.

In April, Junior was released and they both were living together with his sister. Shawneequa was working in the home health care industry towards getting her own place for her children to live with her. During this time, Shawneequa and I would speak on the phone a few times a month; it was never an extended period of time where we didn't communicate.

In the fall of 2019, I hadn't heard from or spoken to Shawneequa and I found it very odd, so I searched for her on social media and called her phone. As the months went by, I became more and more concerned that something was wrong. I reached out to Halim and he hadn't heard from her either. In July of 2020, after more than a year, I received a message on Instagram from Shawneequa and she advised me that she had been in prison for possession of marijuana, possession of methamphetamines and possession of a 9mm handgun. While on a road trip to Texas from Tennessee with Junior, on the way back home, they were stopped by the police. The car was searched and five pounds of marijuana, ecstasy pills and firearms were confiscated. Junior was fresh out of Federal prison and on Federal probation and Shawneequa hadn't been in trouble since the years locked up as a juvenile.

She spent four months in the county jail before being sentenced to two years in prison as a result, but only spent 11 months incarcerated and is currently on parole until August of 2021. In the midst of it all, she still has hope.

As a result of all the emptiness, hurt, pain and abuse, I have been left broken, battered and alone. My life is a result of how I view all I see; I am a 37-year-old cum stain. I have had several incestuous attacks against me that continue to haunt me. I have been married before, yet it didn't have substance because I have been so numb I never allowed myself to feel anything. I gave this man two children, a few black eyes, broken ribs, bruised shoulders and an abuse story with a 106-day stay at a domestic violence shelter. I am constantly trying to escape the stigma of being the wife of a child abuser and possible rapist. I have had intercourse with so many men trying to fill an emptiness that I felt needed to be filled. I desire to be loved, but love is an illusion that eludes me and tells me that I am not good enough, so I am destined to be a side chick. I have fought so hard not to become my mother that I have become just as lost, if not more lost than she is. My children have suffered due to the foundation of chaos; they endured two tours through the CPS/DPSS system because I can't get it right for whatever reason… But, our scars are reminders that the path is real and we no longer live there anymore."

Broken Bird

Dedicated to someone special…

Your story:

Broken
And un-nurtured
Breeds chaotic beginnings
A beautiful young bird, trying so hard to fly
But the question that holds her down is…
Why?
Why doesn't anyone care for me?
Why doesn't anyone love me?
Why do you hurt me?
Why wasn't I good enough?
You can imagine the pain weighing her down
And why flying away is so tough…

Why did he black my eyes
Break my wings?
Why did you shoosh me
When he pushed into me

And I screamed?
Why would you allow me to fix your alcohol
Every time your friends come to visit?
Why did I have to endure the horrors
Of a juvenile prison?

Do you know how hard it was for me to not dream
Of evil things?
Because of what you did with that napkin
I can never enjoy Burger King...
I was alone and empty, suicidal, feeling like life wasn't...
Well life isn't worth living
I can only go to my Creator
Pray for healing power to start forgiving

You didn't break me

My wings will heal
My pain is strength
I know now love is real
The love of my kids
The love of my friends
I no longer look for love in the sexual proclivities of men
So, when you look and see the tears
The ones swimming in my eyes
They're tears of happiness
'Cause love healed this battered bird
Now watch me fly.

Epilogue

I started writing this book in 2013 and it has burdened my soul to release it. I ran into every possible encounter before I mustered up the strength to resume. You see, I don't consider myself a writer, although I have published my work. I meet the subjects of the book and become engrossed in their lives. I don't want to just get a story and print it; I want to fully understand how it is that they ended up in the system. Everyone believes that it is the crimes that got them in prison, but as you have read, their lives were pre-destined long before a crime was ever committed.

As girls, we are raised to be nurturers, lovers, and mothers. As adolescents, we play with kitchen sets and Barbie dolls. We are trained almost instantly to be wives. Oftentimes, this training comes from a single mother, based on a myriad of reasons as to why the homes are broken and fathers are absent. Girls need their fathers for reassurance, love, and validation. When we don't have him, or these qualities in a positive male figure, we seek it subconsciously in other places. I myself have gotten lost in a past relationship and settled for very little just to fill a void, which is a common theme throughout this book.

I founded P.S. Never Give Up Hope Inc. in 2013 to help incarcerated children. I never even thought of focusing on girls, as I mentioned in the prologue. The ton of girls that I have met over the years have helped me in more ways than I could ever name. Every Tuesday for the past 7 years, myself, Ms. Nikki (The Therapist) and Ms. Yolanda (The Yoga Instructor) have gone inside The Detention Center and worked with incarcerated girls to provide literacy, reality therapy, basic yoga, and meditation. We pour all of ourselves into the girls, in the hopes that when they leave us they are equipped with the tools to cope with whatever issues they may be dealing with. We teach them that love truly conquers all and that everything they need is within; they don't need to look anywhere else. It was the girls inside that forced me to write this book because they needed more than we could offer. We have never been incarcerated and many of them were headed nowhere fast, so I had to think quick. Who better to stop young women from going to prison but women who are already there?

This entire experience has been life-changing for me and the girls have a permanent place in my heart. I have met some of the most beautiful souls behind those walls. I learned that you don't have to be in prison to be locked up. Every time I accepted less than I deserve, I was in prison. Every time I was filled with self-doubt, I was in prison. Every time I allowed the enemy to make me forget what God promised me, I was in prison. There are girls all over the world who can identify with the girls within these pages and it has been my steadfast prayer, for years, that their testimonies help you dig deep within and find that little girl that is lost looking for love in all the wrong places—and you tell her that she is loved, important, and valuable.

I thought I would never finish this book and I became discouraged so many times, but after 7 years, I have succeeded. Biblically, God created the world in 7 days. There are 7 days in a week. The Sabbath falls on the 7th day and, finally, 7 is the number of completion. I pushed through death, divorce, and depression because I know that this is so much greater than myself. By the publish date, two more of the girls (Kenitra and Shawneequa) will have been released from prison and one of them back in court fighting for her life (Shara). To the ladies who allowed me to share their stories, as well as those reading this: *P.S. Never Give Up Hope* and remember, *I'm Here For The Girls*. Forever. I love you all!

–Renata

#TheHopeDealer

I'm Here For The Girls…

By: Tiara Walton (also known as Mizhani)

The girls who became women in prison,
Life lessons learned the hard way
The girls who need someone to say,
"I love you and I'm proud"
I'm here to go the extra mile
for the girl that went the extra mile
For the men they loved

The girls who will miss Christmas with the kids
Because they are doing bids
Because they were prisoners of love
Or the lack thereof

For the girls whose father failed to bond,
Now they're coming up with bail
Prison cells, personal hells…
I'm here for you, girl

I'm here for the girl I could have been,
Praying for your heart to heal
Because you weren't given a fair shot
Or a good deal
I don't see your changes,
I see your soul seeking an appeal

I'm here for the girls on this journey
You encountered a situation that changed you
But I beg that you allow it to help you see
That even beyond the walls
People are being saved by your testimony

And if ever the silence overwhelms you
And the nights get too lonely,
Know that God above is only a call away
I pray that you know your prayers are heard

I'm here for the girls
Who needed other girls to hear their story.

Change Comes Now advocates for current and formerly incarcerated women and girls. The organization also supports families that are directly impacted by the criminal legal system. Change Comes Now supplied masks to each and every woman and girl incarcerated in a Florida state prison. It also provided over 15K rolls of toilet paper, thousands of gloves, bars of Dial antibacterial soap and essential hygiene products to include: shampoo, conditioner, deodorant, toothpaste and toothbrushes. All efforts are funded by outside donations and sponsorships. The Founders, Debra Bennett-Austin & Aniesha Austin, have dedicated their lives to the women they left behind the fence.

Change Comes Now will continue to push for change and decrease the female prison population through advocacy, using Participatory Defense as a tool to help give someone a fighting chance to not be sentenced to jail/prison. Parole & Clemency releases are tools in place that are not being utilized. Change Comes Now works directly with the women inside the fence to advocate and support them until they, too, can kiss freedom and join the 'real world'.

Together, out here, Change Comes Now stands to support those left behind, but never forgotten.

Visit changecomesnowfl.org
for more information or to donate.

About the Author

Renata A. Hannans, nationally known as "The Hope Dealer", is a Jacksonville native who earned her B.S. in Social Science from Jacksonville University. Renata's niche for criminal law was discovered at an early age, immediately stemming from her recollection of sitting in on her first trial as a public observer. As a former Case Manager, she was tasked with the responsibilities of guiding at-risk high school students during the pivotal moments of their adolescent years.

Since publishing her first book, *P.S. Never Give Up Hope*, in 2013 she has founded an advocacy organization, P.S. Never Give Up Hope, Inc., focused on reducing recidivism and promoting literacy. Passionate about inspiring youth to strive for their best, Renata enlisted two professional counselors, Yolanda Webster and Shantizia "Nikki" Figgs, to join with her in weekly visits with incarcerated women in the Duval Regional Detention Facility and with teens adjudicated as adults in the Duval County Jail.

There, Renata and her associates engage in guided meditation and reality therapy, as well as reading and discussing books that are diverse and all-inclusive to bridge the gap between illiteracy and incarceration.

Three years ago, Renata partnered with the Honorable Judge Suzanne Bass to create a library in the courthouse where children read a book and write a report in lieu of community service. "If you get lost in the pages of a book, you can go anywhere… There is peace in the pages of a book", she says.

Holding steadfast to her commitment to sharing stories of those who often don't have a voice behind bars, her second book, *I'm Here For The Girls*, focuses on the theme of how men play a role in female incarceration.

Renata has been recognized with several awards for her activist work and community leadership, including but not limited to: READ USA's 2020 recipient of the READ TO HEAL Award, the United Way of Northeast Florida's Sherwood Smith Children's Champion Award and in 2016, she was chosen as a Florida Black Pages Top 20 under 40.

CPSIA information can be obtained
at www.ICGtesting.com
Printed in the USA
LVHW031529220121
677171LV00003B/216

9 780578 815831